LEARNING TO HATE AMERICANS

HOW U.S. MEDIA SHAPE NEGATIVE ATTITUDES AMONG TEENAGERS IN TWELVE COUNTRIES

LEARNING TO HATE AMERICANS

HOW U.S. MEDIA SHAPE NEGATIVE ATTITUDES AMONG TEENAGERS IN TWELVE COUNTRIES

Melvin L. DeFleur & Margaret H. DeFleur

 **MB** Marquette Books
Spokane, Washington USA

Library of Congress Cataloging-in-Publication Data

DeFleur, Melvin L. (Melvin Lawrence), 1923-
  Learning to hate Americans : how U.S. media shape negative attitudes among teenagers in twelve countries / by Melvin L. DeFleur and Margaret H. DeFleur.
     p. cm.
  Includes bibliographical references and index.
  ISBN 0-922993-05-X (pbk. : alk. paper)
  1. United States--Foreign public opinion. 2. Anti-Americanism--Statistics. 3. Popular culture--United States--Public opinion. 4. National characteristics, American--Public opinion. 5. Teenagers--Attitudes. 6. United States--In mass media. 7. Mass media--Social aspects--United States--Statistics. 8. Mass media--Psychological aspects--Statistics. 9. Mass media and youth--Statistics. 10. Public opinion polls. I. DeFleur, Margaret H. II. Title.
  E169.12.D369 2003
  306'.0973--dc22

                                                              2003018277

Marquette Books
2910 E. 57th Ave.
Suite 5, PMB 244
Spokane, WA 99223
509-443-7057
books@cgms.org

CONTENTS

INDEX TO TABLES AND FIGURES, 7

FOREWORD BY DAVID DEMERS, 9

DEDICATION & ACKNOWLEDGMENTS, 11

1. INTRODUCTION, 13

Background, 16
The Central Issues Investigated, 18
Who Designs, Develops and Distributes Media Entertainment Products? 21

2 WHY DO THEY HATE US? 27

The United States as Superpower, 28
The Issue of American Cultural Imperialism, 30
Religion as a Factor, 31
The Contribution of the Negative Incident, 32

3 OBJECTIVES AND OBSERVATIONAL STRATEGIES, 35

Defining and Measuring Attitudes, 36
Defining the "Attitude Object" of the Project, 38
The Likert Scale Items and the Larger Questionnaire, 41
Assessing the Influences of Depictions of Americans in Popular Culture, 41

4 CONTACTING TEENAGERS TO ASSESS BELIEFS AND ATTITUDES, 45

Strategies Used to Administer the Questionnaire, 46
Who Were the Teenagers Studied? 48

5   WHAT WERE THE FINDINGS? 51

An Overview Based on the Combined Data from All Twelve Countries, 51
Profiles of Specific Beliefs about Americans Obtained in Each Country, 55
Responses by Each Country to Each Attitude Statement, 55
Results Obtained from the Media Influences Subscale, 68

6   A MULTI-STAGE EXPLANATION OF MEDIA INFLUENCES, 77

Making a Profit in a Capitalistic Economic System, 78
    The "Invisible Hand" Controlling the Marketplace, 79
    The Problem of "Quality," 80
    The "Inner Man" as "Internal Spectator, 81
The Market: Demographic Characteristics of the Global Audience, 84
Media Dependence on Popular Culture, 88
The Creeping Cycle of Desensitization, 93
Seeking Gratification from Media Entertainment, 94
The Process of Incidental Learning, 96
The Social Construction of Reality, 99
The Gradual Accumulation of Minimal Effects, 103
Putting It Together: A Master Theory of the Effects of
    Mass Communicated Entertainment, 105

7   IMPLICATIONS FOR THE FUTURE, 111

Role of Youth in Acts of Terrorism: A Political Perspective, 111
Terrorism Threats and Stresses on Americans: A Public Health Perspective, 114
Negative Attitudes and the Marketplace: An Economic Perspective, 114
Prospects for Change, 116

INDEX, 123

INDEX TO TABLES AND FIGURES

Table 1. Confidential Questionnaire, 39
Table 2. Correlations Between the Media Influences Subscale and the Attitude Scale, 71

Figure 1. Overall Attitudes Toward Americans by Country, 52
Figure 2. Beliefs About Americans (All Countries, N=1,313), 53
Figure 3. Saudi Arabia: Beliefs About Americans, 56
Figure 4. Bahrain: Beliefs About Americans, 56
Figure 5. South Korea: Beliefs About Americans, 57
Figure 6. Lebanon: Beliefs About Americans, 57
Figure 7. Mexico: Beliefs About Americans, 58
Figure 8. China: Beliefs About Americans, 58
Figure 9. Spain: Beliefs About Americans, 59
Figure 10. Taiwan: Beliefs About Americans, 59
Figure 11. Pakistan: Beliefs About Americans, 60
Figure 12. Nigeria: Beliefs About Americans, 60
Figure 13. Italy: Beliefs About Americans, 61
Figure 14. Argentina: Beliefs About Americans, 61
Figure 15. Americans Are Generally Quite Violent, 62
Figure 16. Americans Are a Generous People, 62
Figure 17. Many American Woman Are Sexually Immoral, 63
Figure 18. Americans Respect People Unlike Themselves, 63
Figure 19. Americans Are Very Materialistic, 64
Figure 20. Americans Have Strong Religious Values, 64
Figure 21. Americans Like to Dominate Other People, 65
Figure 22. Americans Are a Peaceful People, 65
Figure 23. Many Americans Engage in Criminal Activities, 66
Figure 24. Americans Are Very Concerned About Their Poor, 66
Figure 25. Americans Have Strong Family Values, 67
Figure 26. There is Little For Which I Admire Americans, 67
Figure 27. Subscale: Influences of Mass Media Depictions, 70
Figure 28. Population Pyramids, 86

FOREWORD

When foreign graduate students arrive in the United States for the first time, they often tell me that during the first few months here they are very afraid of becoming the victim of a violent crime.

"Why?" I ask.

"Because there is a lot violence in Hollywood movies," they reply. "I thought that's what it would be like here."

Of course, as time passes they realize that their chances of becoming a victim of a violent crime are not extremely high, especially in university communities. The average U.S. citizen has a 1-in-200 chance of being assaulted, forcibly raped, killed or robbed during a typical year. If you factor in the fact that university communities are generally located in low-crime areas, the risk drops even more, probably to less than 1 in 2,000.

"Based on your experience so far, do you think Americans are violent?" I ask the new students.

"No, not really," they often reply. "Most Americans are very friendly."

There's nothing like real-world experience to debunk a myth. But most young people from other countries around the world will never get the opportunity to live in America. For them, the images they derive from U.S. mass media, especially movies and television programs, will be one of the most important sources of knowledge about life in America. And those images, as professors Melvin and Margaret DeFleur point out in this book, are heavily laden with violence and scenes of tough street life in American cities.

No mass communication scholar I know would dispute the notion that Hollywood is partly responsible for the distorted perceptions that many people around the world have of violent crime in the United States. In fact, research suggests that even Americans who watch a lot of television can develop what mass media scholar George Gerbner and his colleagues call a "mean world syndrome"—an exaggerated fear of becoming a victim of crime.

But what if the adverse affects of U.S. mass media didn't stop there? What if young people around the world were developing such distorted perceptions that they thought American women were "sexually immoral"; Americans cared only about getting rich, as opposed to helping the poor; and Americans didn't care about world peace and wanted to dominate everyone in the world? What if young people around the world hated us?

These are some of the questions tackled in this provocative little book. Professors Melvin L. DeFleur and Margaret H. DeFleur asked their foreign graduate students to administer questionnaires to teenagers in 12 countries. Of course, everyone expected distorted perceptions. But the results shocked even seasoned researchers. Teenagers around the world have extremely negative views of Americans—so much so that the DeFleurs conclude they "hate us."

The research data collected by the DeFleurs alone would justify a book on this topic (see Chapters 1-5). But the DeFleurs don't stop there. They provide a detailed theoretical model to explain why there is so much negative imaging in U.S. media and why those images are having adverse effects on young people in other countries (see Chapter 6). In addition, the DeFleurs offer some suggestions for correcting the problem (see Chapter 7).

The DeFleurs do not have all of the solutions to the problem of distorted images of Americans. But that doesn't detract from the contribution that this book makes to an understanding of media effects. Perhaps the most important is that the DeFleurs have drawn attention to a new social problem—one that, if left unresolved, may have dire economic and political consequences for the United States in years to come.

In this post-9/11 world, no public policy maker, governmental bureaucrat or student of international politics can afford to ignore their study or the advice they offer. Now, more than ever, Americans need the support and respect of peoples around the world.

David Demers
Associate Professor and Executive Director
Center for Global Media Studies
Edward R. Murrow School of Communication
Washington State University
Fall 2003

DEDICATION & ACKNOWLEDGMENTS

This book is respectfully dedicated to those international students and their friends, family members and acquaintances in the twelve countries who assisted with gathering the data on which the findings are based. Because some have requested anonymity, their names cannot be revealed. But the authors recognize that without their assistance this project could never have been completed.

We also would like to acknowledge Dr. John J. Schulz of Boston University, who helped publicize the findings of this project by making its Preliminary Report available to journalists worldwide via the Global Beat Syndicate's Web site (http://www.nyu.edu/globalbeat).

Melvin L. DeFleur
Margaret H. DeFleur
College of Communication
Boston University
Fall 2003

CHAPTER 1

INTRODUCTION

The research reported in this book focuses on how mass media and other forms of popular culture help shape beliefs and attitudes about Americans among young people in twelve countries. A total of 1,313 teenagers between14 and 19 years of age (average = 17) responded to a questionnaire that assessed their views of people like you, your family and your neighbors. It was a study of the "next generation" of foreign teenagers and how they feel about people who live in the United States. The countries included Saudi Arabia, Bahrain, South Korea, Mexico, China, Spain, Taiwan, Lebanon, Pakistan, Nigeria, Italy and Argentina. The results show that youths studied in this project have distorted and decidedly negative attitudes toward people who live in the United States.

The major goals of the project were not only to document the nature of teenagers' beliefs about and attitudes toward Americans, but also to provide explanations of how such youthful views are shaped by mass media entertainment products and the long-term consequences of these influences. The central focus of the project, then, is on the role of mass-communicated popular culture in shaping beliefs and attitudes of the next generation that soon will be adults.

Popular culture—that is motion pictures, TV programs, music videos and recordings, as well as other entertainment products—are designed, developed and distributed worldwide by a limited number of multinational corporations. These corporations follow the basic principles of capitalism, as set forth in the late 1700s by Adam Smith. That is, they conduct their activities to make profits—a desirable and applauded goal within the political-economic system of capitalism. Generally speaking, these producers are not deliberately trying to influence anyone's belief and attitudes toward Americans. To maximize profits, their products are designed—logically enough—to appeal to the *largest segment of the market* within the populations of the many countries to which their wares are exported. As will be clear, that segment of the market is the young.

These producers understand completely that the tastes and interests of the young are different from those of the older and more traditional members of populations. In conservative societies, in which the behavior of young people is closely controlled by their elders, youths may conform to such limits. But imported media entertainment allows them vicariously to enjoy the non-conforming behavior depicted—particularly as it portrays young Americans. In many cases, that behavior would be frowned upon, or even be expressly forbidden, within the norms governing their own lives. For that reason, it can seem exciting. Informants from the conservative societies studied in this project have confirmed this observation.[1]

Above all, however, young people the world over want to see *exciting action*. They enjoy seeing explosions, fistfights, car chases, shootouts, criminal activities and other portrayals of dangerous behavior. In particular, young males the world over want to see nude women and graphic depictions of couples in bed. Such experiences and actions are highly unlikely to occur in the realities of their own young lives.

Exactly this kind of exciting content, however, has been increasingly incorporated into the motion pictures, TV dramas, music videos and other forms of popular culture that are produced by media corporations (mostly in the United States) and shipped to other countries. The reason is that competition for audiences among those who produce media entertainment products is *fierce*. Attracting and holding the largest possible audience is critical for financial success. The products produced must attract and hold audience attention. Increasing the excitement level of what is produced enlarges the audience and thereby enhances the profits. Explanations for all of these issues will be provided in subsequent chapters.

A major factor promoting the global distribution of such content is that many societies do not have facilities for producing movies, TV programming or other forms of popular culture that their youthful populations desire. Virtually all, however, have cinemas, radio stations, television broadcasting or cable facilities that serve their populations. In some cases, what is transmitted over these media systems is highly controlled by local government. Even in such societies, some entertainment must be provided. To fill this need, the exported products of the multinational corporations are readily available.

Even if official systems do not provide such content, however, alternative sources are always available. The home use of VCRs and even DVD systems for viewing movies and other content on TV screens is now widespread. Local entrepreneurs the world over quickly obtain copies of the latest films, TV programs and other forms of entertainment. They reproduce them (often as pirated products) and either rent or sell them cheaply in the streets. Government controls are not effective in eliminating this flow of entertainment content.

The consequences of this complex situation, as the present project will show, is that these forms of media entertainment provide subtle but abundant lessons to the youth in societies around the world as to what ordinary American people are really like. After all, they see them depicted daily on their television screens as they view *Baywatch*, *The Sopranos* or *Sex and the City*—or in the local cinema. Thus, they learn what Americans are like when they see their lifestyles, morals and behavior portrayed in TV dramas or movies, or even when they listen to Eminem's lyrics in popular music. The lessons they learn, as the present report will explain, are not planned by those who produce such entertainment products. Moreover, they are learned unwittingly by the young people who enjoy this type of media entertainment.

Essentially, then, the data obtained and reported in the chapters that follow offer evidence that the beliefs and attitudes of the majority of young people in the twelve countries studied have been significantly influenced by such media content and that those views are decidedly negative toward ordinary Americans. Specifically, they have learned that we are *violent, criminally inclined*, and that American women are *sexually immoral.* It is easy to understand, therefore, that Americans are people about whom they should have negative views.

The youth studied have not acquired these beliefs and attitudes by personal contact with Americans—very few have visited the United States. Their views are products of a process that psychologists call *incidental learning*—from subtle and unplanned lessons, learned unwittingly bit-by-bit over a number of years. These lessons about Americans are embedded in movies, TV programs and other content. Simply put, these instructions as to what Americans are like are brought to them by a limited set of global corporations that design, develop and distribute media entertainment products that are eagerly attended to by literally millions and millions of young people word-wide. That process will be repeated to instruct each new generation that comes along.

The present report, then, discusses what kinds of teenagers were studied in the twelve countries to reach these conclusions and how the beliefs and attitudes of these young people were assessed. The report develops a linked set of concise explanations (formal theories) concerning the nature of the system that produces and markets popular entertainment media products on a global basis. It also provides an integrated set of explanations (theories) of what happens when youngsters in various societies encounter representations of ordinary Americans in those products—that is, what they come to believe and how that learning process takes place. Finally, the report sets forth conclusions about the long-term consequences of this complex situation—consequences that are a cause for national concern.

BACKGROUND

Americans today live in a time of stress. Following the attack on the World Trade Center, the news media continue to convey constant, and usually vague, reports of threats of possible terrorist acts to their audiences. Stressful measures to prevent such acts have been put in place at all levels of government. In addition, the relatively recent military actions in Afghanistan and the war in Iraq, with its almost non-stop TV coverage, have added to people's concerns. Violence in the Middle East and elsewhere continues, and from time-to-time individuals said to be terrorists planning violent acts in the United States are taken into custody. Bombings in other parts of the world add still more threatening events.

Taken together, these events have changed people's perceptions of personal and public risk. In many ways, then, all of these shared conditions of concern have generated and now pose what amounts to a significant *public health problem*.[2]

> Immediately after the Sept. 11th attacks, doctors and therapists across the country reported a steep rise in the number of people complaining of anxiety, depression and other psychological problems. ... For people already in treatment, mental health experts said, threats of war and jihad against America have exacerbated symptoms.[3]

Still another source of concern is the "climate of hate" (regarding the United States as a nation) that clearly seems to exist in many countries. Periodically reported by pollsters, it is well-understood that hostile attitudes toward the actions and policies of the United States are held by many of the adults in a number of populations in other parts of the world.[4] These often seem puzzling to Americans, and it can be difficult for ordinary citizens to understand either their nature or their causes.

Those hostile feelings about the United States present a complex picture. Some are related to specific recent military actions by the U.S. armed forces, such as the war in Iraq. Other negative sentiments have existed for a much longer period and have apparently been generated by previous policies and interventions in such places as Somalia, Haiti, Bosnia or Lebanon. Some may be a result of outspoken Muslim religious leaders decrying support of Israel. Still others may be a consequence of complex foreign or economic policies—such as the rejection by the United States of the Kyoto (environmental) Treaty or the proposed (UN) International Criminal Court.

In contrast, and adding to the complexity, are clear indications that at least *some* views of Americans regarding *some* aspects of their culture are *positive*—at least among *some* people in *some* countries. Thus, co-existing with hostile attitudes—at times even in the very same countries and regions, and among the same populations—are favorable assessments of ways of life enjoyed by people in the United States.

For the most part these more positive sentiments concerning particular aspects of the American lifestyles can be found among the young. There is a high degree of interest among youth around the world in American *popular culture*. It is a result of the flow of movies, TV programming, popular music, video games and other media entertainment products from the United States to other countries. Because such media content is so sought after by the young, pictures of popular American entertainers—Elvis, Madonna, Britany Spears and Eminem—can be seen on the walls of their homes, even in countries like Iran and Iraq. The names and the musical styles of these celebrities are familiar to huge numbers of youths in such countries, and for some they serve as role models.

Beyond youthful regard for pop-culture idols, there is among other segments of populations *envy* of the personal, financial, religious and political freedoms that are routinely enjoyed by Americans. In societies where rigid political or religious controls exist, these can seem positive features indeed. Thus, a complex mix of beliefs, views, attitudes and feelings toward the United States, toward the American society and its population can be found in different parts of the world, and even within a particular population.

Because of that complexity, the meaning of terms like "anti-American" or "pro-American" can be difficult to interpret in the various polls and surveys that have been conducted in recent times in countries assumed to be hostile toward the United States. Commonly, it is the *adults* in those countries whose beliefs and attitudes concerning the "United States" have been assessed. There is little doubt that a great many of those adults view the United States in decidedly negative terms. However, much less is known about how young people—teenagers who make up the next generation, as well as the majority of people who live in such societies—feel toward *ordinary Americans*.

This is an important distinction. That is, the official United States is a different "attitude object" than are Americans as people who inhabit the United States. It is the nature of that complexity in beliefs, attitudes, views and opinions, therefore, and the lack of detailed information about the youthful cohort who will soon come of age, that led to the present project.[5]

THE CENTRAL ISSUES INVESTIGATED

Several issues are addressed in the research project that require careful explanation. That is, what *evaluative beliefs*—what appraising assessments, views, understandings and attitudes—do they entertain about individuals and their families who live in the United States? Moreover, are those beliefs *accurate?* Do they reflect the true nature of Americans, or are they *distorted* and *flawed* in ways that provide a basis for negative interpretations and images?

To answer that question, the project assessed beliefs and attitudes toward Americans among more than thirteen hundred teenagers in twelve countries in different parts of the world. Details will be provided concerning how that was done, what was assessed and how barriers to gaining access to teenagers in countries unfriendly to the United States were surmounted. Also explained in the chapters and sections that follow will be what was found, how the results can be interpreted and what their implications may be for American society.

First, however, in order to explain the goals of the project more precisely, an important distinction must be made between Americans *as people* and the United States as an *official entity*. By "ordinary Americans" we mean persons such as you, your family, your friends, your neighbors and the people with whom you work. It is important to understand that is not the same as beliefs and attitudes toward the "United States" as a government. While it is clear that there is widespread hostility among adults in many countries toward the government of the United States—that is, its leaders, policies, power, military actions and so forth—that is not what was studied in the present project. Again, it specifically focuses on teenage views of "Americans" as everyday people.

An important reason for clarifying this issue at length is that some might claim that it is not possible to make a realistic distinction between these different "attitude objects." However, the present authors maintain that it is. Indeed, it is very clear that attitudes toward a government can be completely different than those toward the private citizens that make up its population. Events in the former Soviet Union, and more recent ones in such places as Cuba and North Korea illustrate the point. While the leaders and governments of those countries have been evaluated in very negative ways by most Americans, they have not held parallel feelings about the ordinary inhabitants of those countries.

The case of the hostilities with Iraq in 2003 illustrate the point. Very obviously, the majority of Americans—whether they supported the war or not—truly despised Saddam Hussein and his ruthless regime. At the same time, they were sympathetic and concerned about the majority of decent and private citizens of that country. Indeed, during the conflict, extraordinary measures were taken, supported fully by Americans, to try to protect those people from harm, and then to assist them in getting their lives back in order and to provide for their humanitarian needs.

An important question, then, is whether that familiar *dual pattern* prevails among teenagers in the twelve countries studied in the present project. That is, are their views of Americans, as private citizens *different*, and *more favorable*, than their attitudes toward the United States as an official entity? In other words, do they see the United States in negative terms, but its ordinary people in a more positive way? Or, will the data from the present project show an unusual departure from that dual pattern? That is, will the teenagers have *negative beliefs and attitudes about both*? If that turns out to be the case, it would not fit the dual pattern that commonly prevails among Americans—most of whom hold no negative views of the ordinary people of other countries whose governments they regard in pejorative terms.

Anticipating the presentation of the results from this project, the youths studied definitely do *not* show that typical dual pattern. For the most part, the teenagers studied have quite negative views of *both* the U.S. government *and* of ordinary Americans. Given that outcome, an important question is *why*? That is, *from what sources* have young people in the countries studied acquired pejorative beliefs and attitudes concerning the people who live in the United States? This, therefore, is a second important question addressed in this project. Specifically, an attempt was made to determine whether such negative views have been derived from their *exposure to American popular culture* as discussed above.

That, of course raises the question of *access*. Do teenagers around the world actually have access to and attend to media-delivered content that portrays Americans negatively? There is little doubt that teenagers in almost all countries (except those that live in abject poverty in truly remote areas) have ready access to this type of media-delivered communication. Indeed, they have such access in much the same degree, or in some cases even greater access than is the case with young people in the United States. For example, noted filmmaker Charles C. Stuart traveled extensively in the Middle East in 2003 in order to explore the influence American popular culture was having on Arab identity and the Muslim faith. He found that:

U.S. television programs and movies are pouring into Muslim societies at a dizzying rate thanks to the explosion of satellite networks in the Middle

East—more than 100 today, compared to just one in 1990.[6]

Children in such areas attend the cinema, receive TV programming by satellite, broadcast, cable, or they view VCR tapes or DVDs. They listen to the radio, play video games, purchase records and so on, in much the same way as do teenagers in any American community.

Access to popular culture and entertainment content, then, is not a problem for young people in most countries seeking the experiences of gratification that such products provide. While some governments attempt to restrict access to movies and television content of which they disapprove, in reality that poses few barriers. As explained, virtually any form of popular entertainment can be cheaply rented or purchased almost everywhere on audio or VCR tape, or increasingly on DVDs. These products are supplied by street vendors in virtually every city in the world, regardless of the nature of the government. Local entrepreneurs obtain the media content, often directly from their contacts with Western sources, and then pirate, or otherwise record, and distribute it through their local organizations of vendors. Thus, the same popular music, movies, and television content is readily available to middle-class teenagers in towns and cities in Pakistan, Bahrain or South Korea as it is to young people in New Jersey, Ohio and Oregon.

A third issue to be addressed concerns who prepares and delivers world wide the media content that depicts Americans negatively and why? Answering those questions requires explaining the organization and functioning of the *entrepreneurial system* that designs, develops and distributes the various forms of popular culture that are attended to by young people on a global basis. Specifically, an understanding is needed concerning the ownership, operations and the goals of large multinational corporations that produce and market those products to provide access by youths in almost all countries.

Another truly important issue to be addressed is the *overall nature* of the process by which such content provides youthful audiences with *learning sources* from which they acquire negative and flawed interpretations of ordinary Americans and their ways of life. This is an especially complex issue. It requires an understanding of a series of *stages* by which: (1) global media entertainment content is *shaped*, (2) the way it is *distributed*, (3) why young people *seek it out*, (4) how—lacking other sources—they unwitting *learn* from it, (5) how those lessons slowly *add up*, and (6) how they finally produce seemingly valid—but seriously flawed—*social constructions of reality* concerning the nature of Americans.

Finally, the implications and consequences of what has been found in this project must be considered. What do these results indicate about the complex problems created by current hatred and flawed negative images of Americans among the young people in the countries studied? Are there simple ways to reverse these feelings and bring the youth in such societies to admire and like Americans? That may be the most important issue of all.

WHO DESIGNS, DEVELOPS AND DISTRIBUTES MEDIA ENTERTAINMENT PRODUCTS?

Simply put, a small number of large multinational corporations produce most of the media content consumed on the planet. That includes both news and entertainment. Over the last two decades, there has been a significant consolidation of ownership among those corporations, studios, networks and other organizations that produce, and sell worldwide, motion pictures, television programming, popular music, video games, theme parks and news. As mass communication scholar Yahya Kamalipour of Purdue University states:

> [A] new world is being forged before our very eyes. It is a world in which the mass media conglomerates, such as General Electric, Time Warner, Disney, Capital Cities, ABC and Westinghouse play a significant role in the way(s) that we perceive ourselves, our world, and our fellow human beings. It is a technologically driven, intensely competitive, and corporate-dominated world that was quite unimaginable to our predecessors only a generation ago.[7]

Essentially, then, a small number of organizations, seek profits by preparing, producing and disseminating virtually every form of mass communicated popular culture and media entertainment content. They do so worldwide and have come to dominate both the production and marketing of such products on a global basis.

Media scholars have studied this situation in depth and many argue that these are profit-seeking corporations that operate according to strict business principles—with little concern over the consequences for their audiences of what they produce. Their major objective is to *earn maximum profits* for their owners, shareholders and managers.[8] That is, of course, a laudable goal within the present political and economic system in which such businesses operate. It has not resulted in widespread condemnation of those producers, and it is unlikely that it will. Indeed, few Americans would reject that system for something else.

A lack of concern for consequences is common in many kinds of businesses. Clear examples are the risks to many people resulting from their use of cigarettes, liquor, handguns and fast foods. In such cases, however, the *responsibility for consequences is that of the user*—who is presumed to understand those risks and their potential negative outcomes and be willing to accept them. In these four cases, the risks associated with use of the products have been well-documented. It is widely understood that smoking can lead to lung cancer, that excessive use of alcohol can have serious health problems, that over-indulgence in high-calorie, high-fat food can result in obesity and that handguns can be dangerous to one's health.

In the present case, however, the youth who acquire negative beliefs and attitudes toward Americans by attending to popular culture have no such awareness. The same situation appears to be the case for the producers who offer these products to a young audience. Increases in hostility toward the people who live in the United States is scarcely a desirable consequence. Hopefully, research such as the present project can help to clarify that situation and lead to greater awareness of how that outcome is produced, on the part of both producers and consumers and on the part of the American public at large.

There is another important issue that is *not* addressed in this project, but which deserves comment. It concerns the *news*: Much the same principles, processes and explanations of the effects of popular entertainment content on youth may be applicable to the flow of news from the United States to other parts of the world. The "news values" that are used routinely by gatekeeping editors and others to select and develop their daily agendas of reports in print or broadcasting are well understood. News stories are selected that emphasize crime, conflict, sensationalism, deviant behavior and other actions, situations and events that capture and hold interest among their audiences and readers. They scarcely present an objective picture of life among ordinary citizens in the United States. The goal of course is to increase audience size and therefore profits. Thus, what individuals in other countries see and hear about the people of the United States in news reports also presents a clearly negative picture. Stories of crime, corruption, sex and violence play a prominent role in teaching people about the nature of Americans. For much the same reasons, then, attention to the news from the United States has every prospect of providing the same incidental lessons concerning the characteristics of Americans as is the case with entertainment.

The producers and distributors of the news are largely under the control of the same increasingly limited number of multinational corporations that produce and disseminate entertainment products. However, for some years, the growing consolidation of ownership has created a considerable debate. That debate is not focused on the consequences of negative images of Americans that are so frequently a part of news reports. It has been mainly concerned with the consequence of *limiting diversity* in the reporting of what is taking place. Many critics claim that, as a result of this concentration of ownership, there will be less and less "robust discussion" in the press. Even more alarming, say such critics, views that are contrary to those of the dominant corporations will have a more difficult time being heard.

But even though much the same processes and consequences in shaping views of Americans among those in other countries may be present in the flow of news on a global basis, this issue is not a focus of the present project. As explained, what is of concern here is the nature of what is produced as entertainment in the form of popular culture and how it defines people who live in the United States.

Who are these multinational corporations that have achieved such a presumably powerful position? According to David Demers, the ten most dominant groups (and their latest available sales figures) were: AOL Time Warner, Inc. ($36 billion), Vivendi Universal ($30 billion), The Walt Disney Company ($26 billion), Bertelsmann AG ($16.5 billion), Viacom ($16 billion), The News Corporation ($14.2 billion), Sony ($11.3 billion). National Broadcasting Company ($6.8 billion), The Thompson Corporation ($5.9 billion) and Advance Publication ($4.5 billion).[9] There are others, but taking just these ten together, they earn over $167 billion dollars a year selling media products on the global market—which is more than half of all revenues generated by mass media worldwide.

To whom do they sell all their entertainment products? It is mainly to countries that do not have adequate facilities to produce a sufficient number of motion pictures, television entertainment programs, news reports and other related products to satisfy the desires of their populations. Indeed, *the poorer the country, the more likely it will import virtually all of their mass communication programming and content.* As motion picture attendance, the use of television, VCRs, DVDs, record players and other entertainment technology has come into use worldwide, populations want such products and are willing to pay for them. Even tightly controlled governments have to provide at least *something* and at least tolerate what they can import. For example, Kamlipour notes what he observed during a recent visit to Iran:

> Satellite receiving dishes were prominent on the rooftops of millions of Iranian homes where families would gather around their Sony TV sets and view *Oprah, Donahue, American's Funniest Videos and Growing Pains.* ... movies such as *Dances with Wolves,* and *Silence of the Lambs* were circulating on videocassettes. ... American pop singers, such as Michael

Jackson, Madonna and others (whom I had never even heard of!), were known to the youth.[10]

Thus, the global demand for popular culture entertainment is being filled by a few aggressive conglomerates operating worldwide. However, it would be a mistake to assume that all such media giants are reaping giant profits. Indeed, some are not doing as well as they would like. While there is a huge global market for media entertainment products, it is *an intensely competitive industry*. Indeed, it is so competitive that some of the largest among them are having a difficult time making the profits that their stockholders want. As *The Economist* reported in the summer of 2002, many of their shareholders have been deeply disappointed by their earnings and stock prices:

> Part of the disillusionment reflects gloom over the groups' share prices. The markets have battered the media giants, taking aim particularly at AOL Time Warner and Vivendi Universal. Each of these has had to make vast write-downs of assets bought at inflated prices at the height of the media and Internet bubble.[11]

The fact is, however, that while these groups compete with each other ruthlessly, taken as a whole they have now become the source by which popular media content is delivered to virtually every young person in every country on this planet. They present images and experiences that youthful audiences can get in no other way:

> These images are fed through an array of sophisticated communication networks, particularly the mass media, by the very conglomerates that have penetrated virtually every aspect of people's lives, whether they live in Chicago, New York, Beijing, Tehran, Cairo, New Delhi, Mexico City, Bogota, Moscow, Paris, Algiers, or Johannesburg. In such a market-driven and media-saturated environment, then, it is no wonder, then, to see teenagers in Ankara, Bangkok, Caracas, or other major cities of the world, wearing T-shirts with the imprints of universal or Western icons, such as Michael Jackson, Madonna ... or a myriad of other Hollywood-TV-industry manufactured logos, icons and celebrities.[12]

Generally, then, operating in an intensely competitive environment, in which the demand for popular culture and entertainment products is all but insatiable, a limited number of conglomerates design, develop and deliver mass media entertainment products and various forms of popular culture to truly enormous audiences. The majority of those audiences, due to the demographic structure of human populations, are young people. It is their tastes and interests that must be served in order to achieve as much profit as is humanly possible. For that reason, the corporations are not preparing educational materials that will accurately inform their audiences, and they are not concerned with any possible negative effects or influences that their products may have on those who consume them. As noted, those are not relevant concerns in such a business environment.

The process and consequences involved in this complex situation deserve careful study. While many critics have decried the activities of such corporations from a variety of perspectives, no significant body of empirical research has been developed that provides data on the consequences of the worldwide distribution of popular culture depicting the nature of Americans. While no claim can be made that the present project has no limitations or flaws, it does provide a beginning.

CHAPTER ENDNOTES

1. Many students who came to the United States from conservative countries to pursue degrees in American universities have indicated this to the authors. At home, they were closely governed in what they wore, how they spoke to others, with whom the could socialize and so on. These behaviors were highly controlled by their families and local norms. They reported that when they viewed American family situation comedies (that they saw on TV at home), they were secretly envious of the teenagers portrayed when they saw them talking back to or disobeying their parents, or even dressing in ways not acceptable in their own society.

2. Evidence is accumulating that terrorism acts and threats are posing psychological problems of stress and anxiety among some Americans. For example, a study of more than 1,000 adults in Manhattan indicated that nearly 10 percent of the people studied were having stress disorders. See: Erica Goode, "A Nation Challenged: Mental Health," *The New York Times* (March 28, 2002), p. A-15. Another news article reported a study of 8,300 school children conducted by the Centers for Disease Control and Prevention. The report indicated that thousands of children around the country were experiencing chronic nightmares, fear of public places and other mental health problems following the World Trade Center attack. See: Abby Goodnough, "Pain Found to Linger in Young Minds," *The New York Times* (May 2, 2002), p. A-1.

3. Jonathan Saltzman, "Far from the Front, Cases of Anxiety Rise," *The Boston Globe*, April 6, 2003, p. W-1.

4. An organization that periodically conducts such polls is the Pew Research Center for the People and the Press, located in Washington D.C. It assesses adult beliefs and attitudes toward the United States in many countries, as well as the opinions of local populations

concerning many issues that may be influenced by U.S. policies and actions. Their web site (enter "Pew" as a search term) is simple and easy to use.

5. It is important to understand where the financial support for a project of this type came from. For that reason, a comment is appropriate concerning the background of the researchers, their source of financial support and their reasons for conducting this study. That comment is this: Any study that has potential political or economic implications these days can seem to be suspect in the minds of some. Questions can be raised about who funded the study. What were the goals and motivations of those who supplied the funds? What are the characteristics of the researchers, and how might their commitments and loyalties tempt them to color or slant the results? To set the record clear on these issues, the following facts are in order. No government agency or private group funded this study. The researchers paid all the costs involved from their own pockets. The characteristics of the researchers that might bias their report are these: Both are university professors teaching students from many parts of the world. Neither is a registered member of either political party. Both have served in the Armed Forces of the United States. (Margaret DeFleur served as a medical corpsman during the Viet Nam conflict, and Melvin DeFleur saw extensive combat in the South Pacific as a U.S. Marine during World War II.) Their motivation for conducting the study was to assess the views, attitudes and beliefs about Americans held by the next generation in the countries studied, and to offer the results to those who might make use of their findings to increase the security of the people of the United States.

6. Don Aucoin, "Getting the Picture," *The Boston Globe*, June 30, 2003, p. D 11.

7. Yahya Kamalipour (ed.), *Images of the U.S. Around the World* (Albany, NY: The State University of New York Press, 1999), p. xxii.

8. For a review of scholars who are critical of large-scale media organization, see David Demers, *Global Media: Menace or Messiah?* rev. ed. (Cresskill, NJ: Hampton Press, 2002).

9. *Ibid*, see Chapter 3.

10. Kamalipour, *op. cit.* p. xxiv.

11. See, *The Economist*, "Tangled Webs," May 25, 2002, pp. 67-69.

12. Kamalipour, *op. cit.* p. xxiii.

CHAPTER 2

WHY DO THEY HATE US?

The case for hatred of the United States, its officials, policies and actions, is clear. In recent months observers reporting from many countries have noted much the same phenomenon. President Bush, say some high school students in Germany, is a "second Hitler."[1] Claims are made in some Arabic countries that the tragedy of the World Trade Center was an event planned and conducted by the Central Intelligence Agency in order to arouse hatred against Muslims.[2]

Even twentieth century history is being revised. Some young people in Germany now interpret the World War II bombings of Berlin by the United States and its allies as acts of pure barbarism, carried out by a vicious and immoral nation without any justification.[3] The earlier London blitz and aggressive activities of the Nazis who plundered Europe and conducted the "final solution" for millions of victims have apparently been forgotten.

Perhaps these views should not be surprising. They are held by youths who were born in the last decades of the twentieth century. For them, the roles played by the United States and its allies in the 1940s—liberating European countries from the grip of fascists—can seem little more than dim events in a distant past. For example, today's 17 year olds were born in 1986, nearly half a century after World War II ended—and even after the infamous Berlin Wall came down. Little wonder, then, that they have no active memory and a limited understanding of those events. They regard them as ancient history with few implications for their current lives.

Thus, it appears that what is essentially a "culture of hate" concerning official America has in recent decades been replacing the more favorable views of the United States that characterized earlier generations in various parts of the world. That emerging culture defines the United States in truly negative terms. The evidence is not hard to find. For several years now, night-after-night, Americans have seen on their televisions sets street demonstrations by angry mobs shaking their fists and holding up banners indicating that they "Hate America." Their participants gleefully burn the American flag or set fire to grotesque effigies of the American president. Even more dramatic evidence are the acts of terrorism against American embassies and other assets abroad that have been carried out—as well as the terrible events of September 11, 2001. In some countries, among some people, those acts are seen as deserved and justified.

At the same time, people in other countries do not hate Americans in some blanket sense. Indeed, at least some of them like some features of American life very much—especially the young. But in other ways they despise us. We noted that one source of complexity is that attitudes toward the United States as an official entity are often not identical with their attitudes toward the lifestyle that many Americans enjoy—economic prosperity, along with personal and political freedoms. To many that can seem very attractive. At the same time, the fact that the United States has the most prosperous economy, the most powerful military and one of the most abundant ways of life creates invidious comparisons with the situation of people in many other countries. Those comparisons are seldom a source of contentment.

THE UNITED STATES AS A SUPERPOWER

The question is not whether a culture of hate against the United States exists in some populations. There is no doubt about that. A more important question is *why?* Part of the answer to that question may lie in the current characteristics of the United States as a nation. The most important of those characteristics is undoubtedly its *sheer power*. By the beginning of the 21st century, the United States had emerged as the sole superpower in the world. No other country even approaches its dominance in either military might or economic status. On defense, the United States consistently spends more than a third of the amount spent *by all of the other countries in the world combined* (36.3%). Expenditures by the Pentagon to support the American armed forces will be over $400 billion next year—not including the continuing costs of the war with Iraq—which is greater than what will be spent on their military establishments by the next fifteen most prosperous nations taken together.[4]

In spite of the ups and downs of the stock market, the American economy is still twice that of Japan, which is the second largest in the world.[5] Looked at in another way, the United States has a mere 4.7% of the world's population.

However, in terms of its capacity to produce, its Gross Domestic Product (GDP) is the highest of any country. In recent years the United States produced nearly a third of all goods and services that were created *in the entire world* (31.2%). And finally, the amount invested in research and development (R&D) by Americans annually is close to half that spent by all other nations taken together (40.6%)[6] Given this staggeringly dominant position of military and economic power in world affairs, it is little wonder that it arouses strong, and often negative, emotions of envy and resentment among people in other countries. That is probably inevitable, and it probably will not change over time.

One might be tempted to conclude that such negative judgments could be offset by sentiments of gratitude among some for help in the form of economic assistance, protection, or deliverance from truly oppressive regimes. However, good deeds done in the past do not appear to count for much. The United States, by most objective measures, has been a good world citizen for a very long time. It has helped rid the world of a long list of brutal regimes and dictators, and it has provided both protection and many kinds of financial and other assistance to other nations.

However, there does not seem to be an historical "balance sheet" of such international behavior, by which people in other counties weigh past contributions of the United States against their current grievances. It does not matter much that, during the twentieth century, the U.S. did many things at great cost to its citizens to stop aggression on a worldwide basis, to rebuild nations devastated by war, to stop or prevent the invasions and atrocities in various countries by military actions of aggressors, to return to their people a number of formerly occupied lands and possessions, to supply monetary assistance to nations in economic difficulty, to send food to the starving, and to provide security forces to those in need of peacekeepers.

For the most part, it appears that these efforts brought no legacy of international good will, no long-term appreciation or current public approval, even by those who greatly benefitted. Indeed, among younger generations in many nations—most of whom had no personal experience with these events, or even among those who did—these actions are often forgotten, unknown, or dismissed as insignificant and just dry history.

It is unrealistic to assume, therefore, that such efforts of the past shape the views of people in the present—and especially those of teenagers who make up the next generation. To many Americans, however, it must seem as though Rudyard Kipling had it right early in the 19th century when he noted that he who steps in to help those who need assistance, who have been left behind, or who require protection, will, as he put it:

    ... reap his own reward,
The blame of those ye better,
The hate of those ye guard.[7]

Thus, given the ephemeral nature of remembrances of the past—and America's contemporary position of predominance in economic and military spheres of power—it is not difficult to understand how people in many countries can find something about the United States and its people to *envy, denounce,* or even *hate.*

THE ISSUE OF AMERICAN CULTURAL IMPERIALISM

It is often the case that those in control in another country, or conservative elements in their populations, resent the intrusion into their societies of ideas, role models and moral standards that are not consistent with their traditional ways of life. That raises the issue that some have called "cultural imperialism." It is linked to the distribution of media entertainment and can arouse strong emotions.

The basic charge that Americans engage in cultural imperialism is founded on the idea that cultural change occurs as a result of a *subtle conspiracy* among American business and economic interests, along with the U.S. government. That conspiracy, it is said, seeks to force changes on other people in order to gain economic advantage, political power or some other unspecified form of control over them. This is a popular idea among many academicians as well.

A foundation idea of cultural imperialism is that it brings *change.* There is little doubt that cultures do, in fact, constantly change. Evidence from paleoanthropology and other sources indicates that cultural change has been taking place since the stone age. Various tools, practices, beliefs, ideas and so on have always spread from one society to another. When a population acquires a new product, a new form of conduct or idea, and comes to do something different, it is not always because some outsiders are attempting to force alien practices or material things upon them.

An alternative explanation of change is *cultural diffusion,* which has nothing to do with the powerful seeking domination. For centuries, the spread of untold numbers of innovations from one society to another has been taking place. The American culture as it exists today is a composite of thousands of ideas and practices that had their origins in other societies. Almost every incident of cultural change takes place voluntarily.

In today's highly interactive world, such importations continue at a faster and faster pace. Thus, cultural change is seldom brought about by conspiracies or external pressures exerted by evil business people working with conniving governmental officials. More often they are the result of a voluntary process among a county's inhabitants. When people in a country see an object, idea or practice in another that is not available to them, but which seems appealing and can be acquired from outside, there is often an "adoption of innovation" on the part of local citizens. On their own, they seek and make use of whatever they deem desirable. For that reason there is a constant flow of styles, technologies, foods, language, art and a host of other items between nations.

Nevertheless, some in the receiving countries prefer to see such cultural changes as a consequence of a conspiracy and interpret them as part of a deliberate plan on the part of business and government interests in the United States to gain power and influence. Little wonder, then, that under such conditions, those interpretations generate negative attitudes and even hatred. The adults who hold such views can easily pass them on to their children, perpetuating in the next generation their pejorative beliefs about Americans and the United States in general.

One of the innovations that appears to be most readily adopted among many young people around the world is *popular culture*. Mixed with their views of the U.S. government is their interest in, opinions and assessments of American popular culture as media entertainment. Simply put, there is solid evidence that they may dislike many things about the United States, *but they love its popular culture*. Specifically, they enthusiastically enjoy American movies, television programming, celebrities, entertainers and popular music. As Gary Smith, President of the American Academy in Berlin, recently observed among German youth:

> There is a total disconnect. They wear jeans and listen to Eminem, but this is not relevant to the America that these students are afraid of. In the end it comes down to America's power in the world.[8]

RELIGION AS A FACTOR

Hatred of the United States is often interpreted as a result of religious differences between Muslims and Christians, as well as Jews. These differences have ancient origins. As a religious faith, Islam was founded in the 7th century by the Arabian prophet Muhammed. From its origins in what is now the Middle East, it quickly spread to parts of Asia, Africa and other areas of the world. What brought Islam into conflict with Judaism and Christianity by the 12th century, with beginnings of the Crusades, was its rejection of the basic beliefs that characterized those faiths. Both the God of the Jews, and belief in the divinity of Christ, so central to the beliefs of Christians, were not accepted. Allah, the God of Islam, was said to be all powerful, omnipotent and the only true divinity. Muhammed was his sacred prophet. These differences inevitably brought clashes between Christians and Muslims. In many ways, these differences of beliefs still underlie what is happening between Palestine and Israel today, and they have played a role in attacks on Americans, such as those of September 11, 2001.

Since such conflicts have been present for centuries, they are not likely to go away soon. However, while there is little doubt that religion is a powerful motivating force for many people, those differences do not provide a full answer concerning hatred of Americans. They are a basic source in some cases, but as the present project will show, negative views of Americans and of the United States are not confined to Muslim populations.

THE CONTRIBUTION OF THE NEGATIVE INCIDENT

Beyond the sources of pejorative beliefs and attitudes already suggested, strong emotions may also be a consequence of a *significant negative incident.* These inevitably take place when Americans are present in large numbers on foreign soil. An example is the truly regrettable killing of civilians by U.S. forces in Afghanistan in 2002, in which Air Force personnel flying a combat mission apparently misinterpreted gunfire from the ground (said to have been shot into the air in a traditional way to celebrate a wedding) as anti-aircraft fire. The Americans returned fire with tragic consequences.[9] In objective perspective, the incident appears to have been a "fog-of-war" mistake. For many in the village, however, and indeed in the country as a whole, it was denounced as a barbaric, brutal and deliberate act. Whatever the factual explanation, some found it a focus for hating Americans.

The war in Iraq produced a number of examples—in spite of the fact that Americans tried very hard to use precision weapons to crush a brutal regime that had tortured and murdered thousands, kept the majority in poverty and lived in lavish luxury. Some supposed events probably never happened—such as Iraqi claims in the early phases of the war that an American missile was deliberately aimed at a marketplace in Bagdad—killing a number of innocent civilians. The American military concluded that it was a spent anti-aircraft surface-to-air missile launched by the Iraqis in an attempt to bring down a U.S. plane, but which fell back into and exploded in Bagdad.

Often, the incident is a tragic accident—such as a recent one in South Korea, in which a young girl was run over and killed by a military vehicle. In some cases, the negative incident may be a deplorable criminal act, such as the American soldier who, in recent times, raped a young and innocent girl in Okinawa, a host country. It may even be the loss by a local team in a sporting event, in which some group from the United States participates and wins.

Whatever the realities, and given the fact that negative incidents are almost certain to occur wherever sizable numbers of Americans intervene with intentions to assist in world affairs, it seems imperative to understand the dynamics by which those conditions and events generate hostility.

Most negative incidents are not enough to spark and generate a culture of hate. On the contrary, widespread denunciation of a negative incident by a population appears to rest upon a *prior condition*—a pre-existing complex of negative beliefs and attitudes toward the people of the United States and their government. Thus, a basic assumption upon which the present study rests is this: *The collective condemnation expressed by a people when a negative incident occurs does not come out of nowhere.* As a general principle, a negative incident can become a *cause celebre,* rallying widespread anger, only if a necessary condition is met. Specifically, there must already be in place a foundation of shared negative beliefs and attitudes toward the United States and its people upon which the feelings generated by the specific incident can be based.

It is that assumed necessary condition or principle that in many ways played a part in prompting the present research. We noted earlier that there is little need to demonstrate that the United States is despised in some parts of the globe. Periodic opinion polls and surveys of populations in different countries, carefully conducted by various professional research groups, have shown that many adults in the world have negative, and even hostile, attitudes toward the United States, its leaders, actions and policies.[10]

However, as explained earlier, the existence of those sentiments on the part of adults does not necessarily mean that parallel views are entertained by teenagers concerning the private citizens of the United States. For that reason, it was important to identify in very clear terms what was to be studied in the present project. The question, then, is whether these teenagers *like* the American people who generate these mass communicated entertainment products—movies, television programming, music videos and popular entertainers? Or, do they *dislike* them—sharing the negative views concerning the United States as their older compatriots?

CHAPTER ENDNOTES

1. Nina Bernstein, "Young Germans Ask: For What?" *The New York Times*, March 9, 2003, Sec. 4, p. 3.

2. Jon Sawyer, "Public Anger Against U.S. Runs Deep Even in Egypt, A Close Ally," *St. Louis Post-Dispatch*, September 11, 2002, p. A9; and Robert Mendick, "An Audience with the Tottenham Ayatollah," *Independent on Sunday* (London), September 30, 2001, p. 9.

3. Bernstein, *op. cit.*, p. 3.

4. "Will a Quartet of Euro-enthusiasts Undermine NATO?" *The Economist*, May 3, 2003; Steve Lopez, "Just How Big Does the World's Biggest War Machine Need to Be?" *Los Angeles Times*, May 9, 2003, Metro, p. 1.

5. "The World in Figures," *The World in 2003,* special issue of *The Economist*, pp. 81-87.

6. *The Economist* (reporting figures obtained from the UN, the World Bank, and Institute for Management Development), June 29-July 5, 2002, p. 4.

7. From Rudyard Kipling (1856-1936), "The White Man's Burden."

8. Bernstein, *op. cit.*, p.3.

9. Andrea Stone and Dave Moniz, "Fallout from Afghan Incident Could Be Substantial," *USA Today*, July 2, 2002, p. 6A; Indira A.R. Lakshmanan, "Bomb Kills 11 Afghan Civilians U.S. Calls Airstrike 'Tragic Incident' in Attack on Enemy," *Boston Globe*, April 10, 2003, p. A10.

10. See, For example: "We Have to Take Muslim Anti-Americanism Seriously," *Newsday*, March 26, 2002, p. A35; "Poll on Islamic Mood Isn't Surprising," *USA Today,* March 4, 2002, p. 11A; "Even the Kuwaitis Dislike Us," *Pittsburgh Post-Gazette*, May 29, 2002, p. A9; "Life, Liberty and the Pursuit of Division," *The Times* (London), July 4, 2002.

CHAPTER 3

OBJECTIVES AND
OBSERVATIONAL STRATEGIES

Because of the complex and multidimensional nature of the views, opinions, beliefs and attitudes toward Americans, as well as toward the U.S. government, it is essential to clarify the objectives of the present project. Explanations are also required to understand the strategies used to obtain the quantitative findings. A major reason for doing so is that not everyone is familiar with how such a project is conducted, and the way in which psychologists define attitudes. Moreover, there are a great many ways in which they go about measuring such attitudes and the implications of what is found can sometimes be less than clear.[1]

First, what are attitudes and how are they measured?[2] The measurement strategy used in the present project makes use of a classic procedure originally developed by psychologist Rensis Likert in 1932.[3] With numerous modifications since then, the Likert Scale has become one of the most widely used means for measuring attitudes in contemporary times. It is a complex procedure. For that reason, the discussion that follows makes no assumption that its nature is either obvious or well understood.

To begin with, this study assessed the attitudes of teenagers toward ordinary Americans as an attitude object. This immediately raises two questions: Exactly what is meant by the term "attitude," and what can kinds of things, events or other phenomena can be designated as an "attitude object?" Providing specific answers to these questions may sound unnecessary, but anyone familiar with the voluminous psychological literature on the nature of attitudes and the part they play in shaping behavior will recognize that these concepts have been defined in a great many, and sometimes contradictory, ways.[4] Therefore, because the term "attitude" can mean many things to many people, it is necessary to describe how this concept was defined and measured in the present project.

DEFINING AND MEASURING ATTITUDES

The term "attitude" needs definition in such a way that it lends itself to the *strategy of measurement* that will be used. Therefore, for the purposes of the present project, the following serves as a general definition:

An attitude is *a configuration of related evaluative beliefs about some attitude object.*

Stated in that way, the definition identifies an attitude as a "cognitive" condition—that is, a state of "thinking, believing and feeling" that characterizes an individual. At the same time, of course, that definition raises two additional conceptual questions: (1) What is an *evaluative belief*? And (2), what is an *attitude object*?

Here, the answers are relatively simple. An evaluative belief about something is one that implies *acceptance or rejection*, that is, a *positive or negative* assessment of the attitude object. Or, put more simply, a *favorable versus unfavorable view* concerning that object.

To illustrate, assume that the task is to assess people's attitudes toward a particular city, such as *Boston,* as an "object" about which a person can have positive or negative beliefs. One could, of course, have a belief that "Boston is a city in Massachusetts," or "Boston has a large population." Both of those statements express beliefs that a person might hold, and both happen to be true. However, both are simply statements of *fact* and if a person agreed with them that does not imply that he or she has a favorable or unfavorable orientation toward or Boston as an attitude object.

In contrast, statements such as "I like Boston,"or "Boston is a nice place to live," do have such evaluative dimensions. If a person "agreed" with these statements, it would imply that he or she entertains at least *some* level of a favorable or positive orientation toward the city. If that same person "strongly agreed," it would suggest an even greater level of positive feelings. The opposite would be true if the person "disagreed" or "strongly disagreed" with the statements. This level of agreement or disagreement (e.g. "agree" or "disagree" vs "strongly agree"or "strongly disagree"), then, indicates two different levels of positive or negative feeling.

Those simple considerations concerning the nature and level of evaluative beliefs provide the basis of the Likert Scale strategy for assessing a person's attitude toward such an "attitude object." One can prepare a *list* (say a dozen or so) of related evaluative statements toward Boston—half expressing a negative proposition and half a positive one. If a person whose attitude is being assessed shows a consistent pattern of "agreeing" or "strongly agreeing" with the positive statements in that list, and "disagreeing" or "strongly disagreeing" with the negative ones, that pattern provides *observable evidence* of his or her underlying views, feelings and beliefs (that is attitude) about that particular "attitude object."

An advantage to this strategy is that it is not difficult to "quantify" such attitudinal responses. In the standard Likert procedure, if a subject chooses a response category, such as "agree" for a particular statement that expresses a *modestly favorable* view, that response can be given a positive number (such as a score of +1 for that statement). If the person's choice indicates an *even more favorable view* of the statement, such as "strongly agree," that can be assigned a score of +2. For negative responses the same strategy can be used. Modest and strong negative responses would receive corresponding numbers of -1 and -2. Neutral responses would receive scores of zero.

In developing the Likert attitude scale for the present project, however, a common and very simple variation on this procedure was used to obtain numerical scores for responses. The purpose was to make the results easier for non-specialists to understand, and to simplify the task of representing them in charts (as will be seen in the presentation of the results in later sections). Using this variation, a numerical transformation of the -2 through +2 numbers was performed by multiplying each by a constant factor. In this case, that constant was 2.5. This provided individual attitude scores for each of the responses to the statements in the scale that ranged from -5 (for very negative responses) through +5 (for very positive responses), with zero representing the mid-point (neutral responses). Again, this numerical transformation does not change the procedure or the results in any way, other than to make them easier to understand and to represent graphically. (These numbers will be found at the bottoms of the numerous charts presented in later sections.)

When a particular subject has responded to each of the statements of evaluative belief—by selecting a response category for each that expresses his or her view—then the positive or negative scores corresponding to those responses can be averaged over the total number that make up the attitude scale. This provides a single number representing that person's internal psychological orientation (a favorable or unfavorable view) toward the attitude object.

Obviously, the scores for all subjects assessed in a particular country can also be averaged to obtain an "overall" attitude measure for all subjects from that country.

But, given that measurement strategy, let us return to the question of what specifically is actually meant by an "attitude object?" We used "Boston" in the explanation above, but the idea of an attitude object is quite flexible. An attitude object for a person can be *any aspect of his or her physical or social environment about which he or she has positive or negative feelings* (that is, evaluative beliefs). Examples of such "objects" would be particular *categories of people* —such as Catholics, old people, Muslims, lawyers, movie stars or ex-convicts. They might be *political decisions*—such as passing new taxes or undertaking military action against some country. Another "object" might be *public policies*—such as those of affirmative action, same-sex marriage or allowing or preventing abortions. Or, the object could be various *forms of human conduct*—such as using drugs or engaging in political protest. These are only a few examples of possible attitude objects about which people can have configurations of positive or negative evaluative beliefs.

In summary, a decision was made to define attitudes in the traditional way as a set of evaluative beliefs (about an attitude object) making it possible to use a Likert Scale. This procedure makes use of a set of statements of evaluative beliefs about an attitude object, and it provides a numerical (positive or negative) score for each statement by a subject or respondent. After the numerical transformation explained, those scores were averaged to obtain an attitude score for each teenager. Those were then averaged for each country. This permitted both statistical analyses of the results and the preparation of tables and charts that present the results in an easy-to-understand manner.

The Likert Scale developed in this project to assess teenagers' attitudes toward ordinary Americans is shown in Table 1. These twelve statements were composed after extensive discussions—using focus group strategies—with graduate students who had recently arrived at Boston University from each of the twelve countries studied in the project. The statements reflect the beliefs that many of these students felt were common among the young people they knew at home—other youths who had neither traveled to the United States nor had any extended contact with Americans.

DEFINING THE "ATTITUDE OBJECT" OF THE PROJECT

A factor that complicated the designing of the objectives and strategies of the present project was the fact that in recent years there have been many reports in the press concerning "attitudes toward America," or "attitudes toward the

TABLE 1

CONFIDENTIAL QUESTIONNAIRE

Concerning Your Opinions About Americans

Read each of the statements below. Note the phrases above the lines of small spaces [ ] for each of the statements. After reading the statement, decide how you feel about what it says concerning **most Americans** (that is, citizens of the United States).

If you "strongly agree" with the statement, then put an X in the small space [ ] under that phrase. If you "strongly disagree," place the X in the space under that phrase. If your feelings are somewhere in between, or you are undecided, write the X in the space that best expresses how you feel.

Question	I Strongly Disagree	I Disagree	I Am Undecided	I Agree	I Strongly Agree
1. Americans are generally quite violent.	[ ]	[ ]	[ ]	[ ]	[ ]
2. Americans are a generous people.	[ ]	[ ]	[ ]	[ ]	[ ]
3. Many American women are sexually immoral.	[ ]	[ ]	[ ]	[ ]	[ ]
4. Americans have respect for people unlike themselves.	[ ]	[ ]	[ ]	[ ]	[ ]
5. Americans are very materialistic.	[ ]	[ ]	[ ]	[ ]	[ ]
6. Americans have strong religious values.	[ ]	[ ]	[ ]	[ ]	[ ]
7. Americans like to dominate other people.	[ ]	[ ]	[ ]	[ ]	[ ]
8. Americans are a peaceful people.	[ ]	[ ]	[ ]	[ ]	[ ]
9. Many Americans engage in criminal activities.	[ ]	[ ]	[ ]	[ ]	[ ]
10. Americans are very concerned about their poor.	[ ]	[ ]	[ ]	[ ]	[ ]
11. Americans have strong family values.	[ ]	[ ]	[ ]	[ ]	[ ]
12. There is very little for which I admire Americans.	[ ]	[ ]	[ ]	[ ]	[ ]

United States." Some have been impressionistic observations of populations in different countries around the world provided by journalists, visitors, former residents, or other informants. Many are colorful accounts about how "people in the street" in those countries feel about the "United States" or about "Americans."

There are several problems with such reports. They do not carefully define the attitude object; it is not always clear who was being observed; they are not based on careful measurement and they are often contradictory. For these reasons, such impressionistic accounts offer a very confusing picture and they are of limited value for assessing how people in other countries actually view people who live in the United States.

Beyond those reports, there is also a large number of well-conducted and large-scale studies by professional pollsters of the beliefs and attitudes of specific populations concerning the United States, or Americans, as attitude objects in different parts of the world. Many show increasingly negative attitudes toward the United States.[5]

Unfortunately, these different reports and polls have two limitations in terms of the objectives of the present project. First, for understandable and logical reasons, they sample adult populations rather than youth. In addition, these polls, taken as a whole, present a confusing picture because they are based on different measurement strategies and have focused on different aspects of U.S. policies, cultural products, official actions, etc. In trying to sort out specifically what these different "attitude objects" were, there appear to be at least three distinct topics to which most of these reports were referring. Specifically, they were the following:

- *Attitude Object 1:* The United States as a political, economic and military power.
- *Attitude Object 2:* American popular culture and mass media entertainment products.
- *Attitude Object 3:* American political freedoms, technology and financial advantages.

Among those who write about, conduct polls about, or publicly comment on, beliefs about the nature of the United States and American life as viewed by populations in other countries, most appear to focus on Attitude Object 1. These assessments seem clearly to indicate that the views of the people studied are largely *negative* toward the United States, in terms of its leaders, policies and actions.

A number of polls have on some occasions assessed views concerning Object 2. Here a mixed picture has emerged. Entertainment products and popular culture developed in the United States are viewed by many adults in conservative countries in a negative way. Among religious leaders, and others in such societies, the content of such imports is often seen as having a corrupting influence on youth—bringing to their attention unwanted ideas, behavioral models and moral codes. At the same time, other sources claim that young people (in particular) have *overwhelmingly favorable* attitudes toward Object 2. They base that claim on the grounds that such youngsters enjoy and highly approve of popular music, celebrity performers and other entertainment products that are produced in the United States.

However, in discussions with people who have traveled within, or have lived for a time in various countries, Attitude Object 3 is frequently cited as evidence that *favorable* attitudes toward Americans prevail. They report that there is often wistful envy of the democratic system, the personal freedoms and the affluent lifestyle that they believe many Americans enjoy. With tongue in cheek, such informants report, local people in such countries essentially say, "Yankee go home," but then quickly add, "But take me with you!"

As explained, Objects 1, 2 and 3 were *not* what was studied in the present project. The focus of the study was on another and different attitude object —*the daily behavior, standards of conduct, and moral codes of ordinary Americans and their families.*

Basically, then, three major questions are addressed in this project. One is to assess the complex dimensions of beliefs and attitude objects that teenagers in other countries appear to have concerning the people who live United States. A second is to try and unravel the sources from which they obtained their beliefs and attitudes. A third, which will be explained in greater detail, is to discuss and explain the implications of what was found.

THE LIKERT SCALE ITEMS AND THE LARGER QUESTIONNAIRE

To accomplish the project's objectives, twelve evaluative statements were prepared for the Likert scale to assess the overall attitudes toward Americans of the youthful respondents (see Table 1). The scale was included in a larger questionnaire that gathered data on patterns of TV and VCR ownership, movie attendance and other media use; travel to the United States; and personal characteristics. Each, of course, was carefully translated into the language of the country where the teenagers lived, and was thoroughly checked by translators in each country to ensure it would be understood by the respondents.

ASSESSING THE INFLUENCES OF DEPICTIONS OF AMERICANS IN POPULAR CULTURE

There are no simple answers to the complex question of the sources of anyone's attitudes, actions or beliefs concerning any issue or object in their environment. The roots of teenage negative views of Americans can be many.

However, it is not difficult to make a case that media entertainment content plays a significant role. Teenagers are heavy users of mass communicated entertainment and popular culture. Going to the cinema is a frequent activity of young people in all of the countries studied. Furthermore, music recordings, radio and television broadcasts are almost universally available.

If movies, popular music and television programs are not produced locally, they have to be imported. However, not many countries have such production facilities and they must obtain entertainment products for their populations from those that do. Remarkably, few governments rigidly censor all that is made available to their populations. Indeed, on the evening in which the "shock and awe" bombing campaign began in Bagdad in April of 2003, the local (Iraqi government operated) television broadcast system was showing an American movie (*The Guilty*). That particular film contains a great deal of controversial violence and sexual content.

Even if the media are rigidly controlled by governments, previously recorded programming is easily obtained via VCR tapes or DVDs that are sold or rented on the streets. With those in place, something of interest will always be readily available to young people seeking entertainment.

It is easy to understand, then, that entertainment products, particularly in the form of TV programs and movies, are obtained from Western sources and distributed in one way or another to a great many local populations. To underscore this factor of availability, an effort was made in the present project to determine the degree to which television sets and VCRs were in use in homes and elsewhere (e.g., community and village centers) in the countries studied. As it turned out, television receivers and equipment for playing VCR tapes were virtually universal in the homes, the homes of friends or elsewhere, providing ready access for the teenagers who participated. That may not be true of the desperately poor in less developed societies, but people in the middle economic strata of the twelve societies studied commonly enjoy these facilities.

To gain information on the possible influence of mass-communicated entertainment products on the attitudes of the youths studied, the Likert Scale that was used provided a way in which to assemble data on this topic. The strategy used is what psychometricians call a *subscale*. A subscale is a "measure-within-a-measure." It is based on a small number of the items (evaluative statements) that are embedded within the overall Likert scale. In the present case these were items 1, 3 and 9 (emphasizing violence, crime and sex). These were included because they represent the most common themes that the producers of media entertainment use to make their products interesting and exciting for their audiences. Scores obtained from this subscale provided information about influences of *depictions of Americans in mass media entertainment content* (e.g., mainly movies and televison programs) as sources for the views of the respondents. Additional items included in the larger questionnaire to which the subjects responded focused on the *access* the subjects had to media entertainment, whether they or their families had traveled to the United States, and their personal characteristics in terms of age, gender, etc.

In general, then, the overall objective of the investigation can be stated simply. It is to gather, analyze, present and interpret data provided by a Likert attitude scale, as well as information from the larger questionnaire, responded to by teenagers in twelve countries around the world. As noted, one strategy for achieving that objective was to use a subscale to study the influences of certain features of media entertainment content that define Americans in negative ways.

Finally, the project's overall objective includes an effort to understand and explain the major stages in the complex process by which such media entertainment is developed, distributed and consumed to produce flawed views of Americans among young people in other countries. Stated in formal terms, the project seeks to:

(1) Understand the ways in which the next generation in the countries studied regards Americans. That is, an important goal is to measure attitudes and beliefs about ordinary Americans held by teenagers in those countries who will soon become politically and economically active adults.

(2) Try to understand the many sources from which such views are formed—with a particular emphasis on the part played by depictions of American families and individuals, including their behavior and ways of life, in motion pictures, television entertainment and popular culture.

(3) To describe the complex process by which media content and other popular culture is designed, developed and disseminated to teenage audiences in countries around the world, as well to explain the process by which they attend and learn about Americans from its content.

CHAPTER ENDNOTES

1. Melvin L. DeFleur and Frank R. Westie, "Attitude as a Scientific Concept," *Social Forces*, 42, 1, 1963, pp.17-31. See also: Melvin L. DeFleur and William R. Catton, "The Limits of Determinancy in Attitude Measurement," *Social Forces*, 25, 1957, pp. 295-300,

and: Melvin L. DeFleur and Frank R. Westie, "Verbal Attitudes and Overt Acts: An Experiment with the Salience of Attitudes," *American Sociological Review*, 23, 6, 1958.

2. For a comprehensive explanation of the nature of attitudes, their measurement and related issues, see: Stuart Oskamp, *Attitudes and Opinions* (Englewood Cliffs, NJ: Prentice-Hall, 1991).

3. Rensis Likert, "A Technique for the Measurement of Attitudes," *Archives of Psychology*, No. 140, 1932.

4. The debates over the nature and psychological functions of attitudes began more than a century ago. Literally thousands of studies on different types and aspects of attitudes have been published over the years. For examples, see: Melvin L. DeFleur and Frank R. Westie, "Attitude as a Scientific Concept," *Social Forces*, 42, 1, 1963, pp.17-31. See also: Melvin L. DeFleur and Frank R. Westie, "Verbal Attitudes and Overt Acts: An Experiment on the Salience of Attitudes," *The American Sociological Review*, 23, 6, 1958, pp. 667-673.

5. Examples are the complex and detailed reports developed by the Washington D.C., Pew Research Center. Beliefs, opinions and attitudes of 38,000 people in 44 nations were studied in 2002 and another 16,000 a year later (following the war in Iraq). Their views of many attitude objects were assessed, including the following: economic globalization, democracy, terrorism, the United States and a number of others. Opinions regarding the United States have become increasingly negative. Not studied were attitudes toward the common people of the United States. See: "What the World Thinks in 2002," The Pew Research Center for the People and the Press, Washington, D.C., December 4, 2002. See also: "America's Image Further Erodes, Europeans Want Weaker Ties," The Pew Research Center, March 18, 2003.

CHAPTER 4

CONTACTING TEENAGERS TO ASSESS BELIEFS AND ATTITUDES

Using high school students as subjects for research is difficult in any country. Even in the United States, gaining permission for classes of high school students to respond to a questionnaire can be problematic and complex. To accomplish this in the United States, approval must be obtained from the educational administrators in charge of the school. In addition, cooperation must be sought from the teachers in charge of specific classes. Moreover, permission often must be obtained directly and in writing from the parents of the students involved.

In other words, school administrators, teachers and parents (understandably) are very cautious about what kind of research questionnaires they will allow young people to complete. Particularly difficult is parental permission. The reason is that trying to contact youthful subjects or their parents, by calling on families at home, can be a challenge. Sampling frames—that is, lists of families who have children of the specific age and student status required—are seldom available. Even if such lists can be obtained, parents may or may not cooperate.

In the setting of nations *not* friendly to the United States, gathering such permissions from all the authorities and parents is "mission impossible." Indeed, in the present case, such a strategy could not be accomplished. That is, it would have meant obtaining permission from educational officials through twelve different diplomatic channels in order to access young people in their high schools to serve as subjects in an assessment of attitudes toward Americans. Even with an unlimited budget, gaining governmental and family permission in such diverse settings would have posed unsurmountable problems.

To overcome these barriers, the authors decided to use a different strategy to gather the data. They were able to employ an "under the radar screen" approach that by-passed government officials and relied instead on educators in each of the countries studied. At the same time, there was no intent to use subterfuge or deceptive measures to avoid contact with government officials.

STRATEGIES USED TO ADMINISTER THE QUESTIONNAIRE

How were the data gathered? That is, how was the questionnaire presented to the youthful subjects in order for them to record their responses?

Essentially, it was done through a network of contacts with friends and relatives within the countries studied—persons who were willing to administer the questionnaire to the young people the authors wanted to study. These arrangements were made in 2002 through a network of interpersonal friendships and family relationships existing among graduate students studying in the United States who were from the countries involved. These were students who were in advanced degree programs in a private northeastern university. The key element was that each had friends and/or relatives who were teaching in, or administering, high schools in the specific countries.

To make the arrangements, one or more nationals (graduate students) from each country, working with the authors, identified and contacted specific friends or relatives by email or phone. Each of these was a classroom teacher or principal in a high school in their home countries. In each of the 12 countries, these persons were asked by the student participants if they would be willing to assist personally with data-gathering in their school's classroom settings.

These were not simple requests. Some refused. In addition, some of those contacted were concerned about possible retaliation if their attempt to assist Americans was revealed. Even among those who had no such concerns, serious questions were raised about the purpose of the study and its sponsors. There were, of course, suspicions as to who was doing this and why. When the nature and goals of the project were clearly and fully explained—as university research, and not spying by the CIA or some other agency of the United States—the majority of these relatives, friends and acquaintances were very cooperative, even in some cases with risks to themselves.

Clearly, a significant issue in some of the countries was the assurance of total anonymity for both the youthful subjects and those who assisted with data-gathering. When the procedures for assuring that anonymity were made clear, in each setting those associates who participated were both interested and curious about what the results would show. Therefore, the result was that all of the questionnaires were personally administered in classrooms by active teachers and high school administrators in each of the twelve different countries in 2002.

While this strategy made data-gathering possible, it had obvious technical sampling limitations. At the same time, however, it also had an important advantage. Those who administered the questionnaires in the classrooms were persons who were familiar to the subjects. They were not strangers to be distrusted—who might be seen by the teenagers as agents of the United States. This was a serious issue, and as noted, some who helped to administer the questionnaires, were truly concerned that their identities not be revealed. They had legitimate concerns about potential negative reactions by their governments. For that reason, no additional information on this feature of the methods will be provided. What did take place, however, was that the completed questionnaires were filled out seriously and responsibly, and they were returned in a timely manner to the authors for analysis.

As is the case in any psychometric measurement, the authors were concerned about *validity*—whether the procedure used actually assessed what it was designed for. There is always the danger that respondents might deliberately try to mislead the investigator, or that they may have filled out the questionnaires in capricious ways. That turned out not to be the case. There are reasons to conclude that the teenagers found the experience an interesting one and that they completed them responsibly. Evidence for this conclusion comes from the fact that many of the young respondents wrote extended remarks to indicate that they welcomed the experience of having their views sought. Indeed, some filled entire backs of several pages. Allowing youths to express their views is not common in some of the countries included in the project. This led some of the young subjects to state in detailed notes their appreciation for this opportunity to explain how they felt. Other respondents added extended explanations that elaborated upon what they had recorded for various items in the Likert scale.

Some of the teenagers prepared crude scatological drawings in margins or on the backs of pages that offered suggestions that Americans should perform a gross but anatomically impossible act on themselves. Still others expressed clearly in short essays their strong dislike of Americans. But more important, there was no significant evidence of attempts to fool the researchers or to play games (such as leaving many items blank, or checking the same response category in the same way for all items, etc.).

WHO WERE THE TEENAGERS STUDIED?

What were the characteristic of these subjects? As indicated, they were teenagers who were in high schools. Even so, the nature of school systems is not the same from one country to another. What Americans think of as "high school" may be defined somewhat differently in other countries. As it turned out, this was not really a problem. To achieve as much comparability as possible, it was made clear to those administering the questionnaires that the respondents needed for the study should be in schools that were *beyond the primary level, but not at the college level.* In each case, these were schools attended by young people who were in their early to late teens.

Their median age was 17 years—with half above that age and half below. They were evenly divided between males (51%) and females (49%). Few had ever traveled to the United States (11%) and those who had were primarily from the Western and more developed societies. Virtually all, however, often attended the cinema and viewed programs on TV (most of which were produced in the United States).

In social class terms, the teenagers were neither the rich nor the poor, but those basically in the middle level of their societies. Those who assisted locally with data-gathering were asked to make certain that the schools selected were neither elite and expensive institutions attended by the children of the wealthy nor humble ones attended by the very poor. Explanations and descriptions provided by those assisting indicates that these criteria were carefully applied. Only in one case were the questionnaires that were returned to the authors not used in the analysis. This was because they were from a private and expensive school catering to the children of the wealthy. Similarly, none of the questionnaires came from schools for the very poor.

Overall, then, each of the schools selected served youths from the *middle* to *lower middle* socioeconomic strata in the societies under study. While these categories are defined somewhat differently in each of the countries, the parents of the students who responded are generally people whose heads of family are literate, steadily employed, of at least modest means, and who are supportive of their children's education.

Obviously, this was not a routine sampling procedure. This project's samples do not meet rigorous text-book criteria of equal probability by random selection from a carefully defined and pre-listed population (sampling frame) of subjects. Meeting those requirements was simply not possible. Essentially, then, these are twelve *convenience* samples. They also have some features of *quota* samples as well. But whatever their definition, their selection was based on the above procedures and criteria.

The result was an overall sample of 1,313 reasonably comparable teenagers from the twelve countries involved. Their responses provide a wealth of insights about how such youths feel about Americans in different parts of the globe. In the opinions of the authors, it seems likely that their views are at least somewhat representative of the young people in the middle levels in each of the countries studied.

CHAPTER 5

WHAT WERE THE FINDINGS?

The principal findings on the attitudes of these 1,313 teenagers are presented in three major sections that follow. The first section presents two sets of results: One set is from *all countries combined*. This is followed in this first section by the more detailed results on each of the attitude scale items *from each country separately*. The second major section on results presents the findings in a different way—*item-by-item from the attitude scale*, with the results from each country listed in rank order. Finally, the third section on findings is devoted to the results from the *media subscale.* Immediately following, then, is a summary of the results from the first of these three analyses.

AN OVERVIEW BASED ON THE COMBINED DATA
FROM ALL TWELVE COUNTRIES

Figure 1 shows the average or *overall attitude score* for the respondents in each of the countries, in rank order. Figure 2 lists the average responses for all countries for each item. The significance of these charts is that they provide for comparisons of the overall views of Americans among the twelve countries studied. As can be seen, in most of the countries, the respondents had at least some degree of negative attitudes toward American people. These range from clearly negative averages in Saudi-Arabia and Bahrain, through essentially neutral views in Nigeria and Italy. The only respondents who had somewhat positive attitudes were the young people in Argentina.

It should come as no surprise that teenagers in Saudi-Arabia and Bahrain—two Muslim countries—have quite negative views of Americans. The

Figure 1
Overall Attitudes Toward Americans by Country

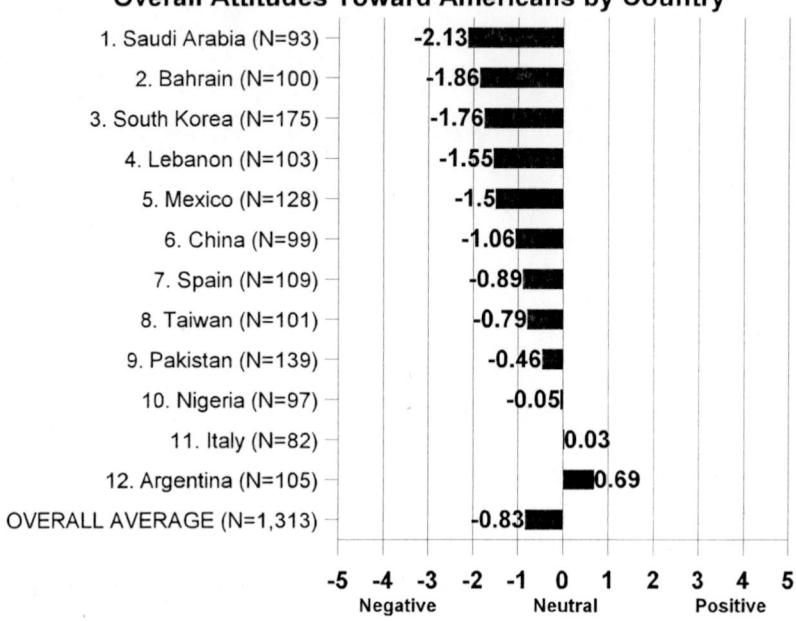

1. Saudi Arabia (N=93)	-2.13
2. Bahrain (N=100)	-1.86
3. South Korea (N=175)	-1.76
4. Lebanon (N=103)	-1.55
5. Mexico (N=128)	-1.5
6. China (N=99)	-1.06
7. Spain (N=109)	-0.89
8. Taiwan (N=101)	-0.79
9. Pakistan (N=139)	-0.46
10. Nigeria (N=97)	-0.05
11. Italy (N=82)	0.03
12. Argentina (N=105)	0.69
OVERALL AVERAGE (N=1,313)	-0.83

-5 -4 -3 -2 -1   0   1   2   3   4   5
Negative   Neutral   Positive

influence of religion is often cited to account for such negative feelings. However, it is likely that the negative image of Americans also reflects what psychologists refer to as a "halo effect." That is, a carry-over influence from the beliefs and attitudes of the widely held-views of adults in those countries concerning the U.S. government, its official policies and actions. A recent Gallup poll of the opinions held by adults in nine Muslim countries, concerning the official actions and policies of the United States government, showed very negative attitudes.[1] It seems most likely that those adults have a significant influence on the next generation, passing on their views, not only about the official policies and actions of the United States, but also—in a halo effect—about Americans as people as well.

What is surprising about Figure 1 is what was found in South Korea and Mexico. The young respondents in both countries held attitudes toward Americans almost as negative as those in Saudi-Arabia and Bahrain. Without considering the influences of mass communications, it would be hard to explain why young people in South Korea and Mexico judge Americans so harshly.

These negative judgments are not solely a function of religion. Neither Mexico nor South Korea has a significant Muslim population. The case of South

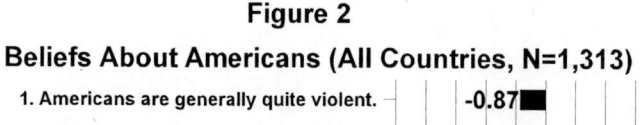

Figure 2
Beliefs About Americans (All Countries, N=1,313)

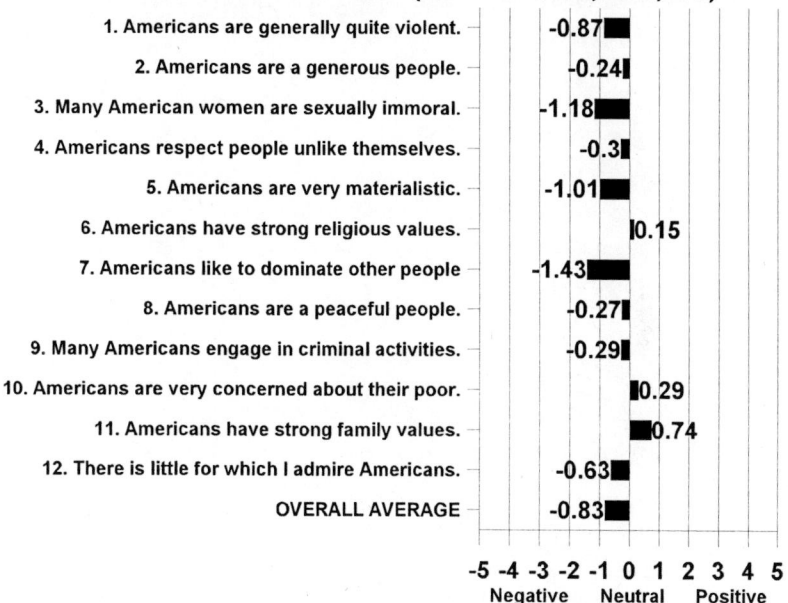

1. Americans are generally quite violent.	-0.87
2. Americans are a generous people.	-0.24
3. Many American women are sexually immoral.	-1.18
4. Americans respect people unlike themselves.	-0.3
5. Americans are very materialistic.	-1.01
6. Americans have strong religious values.	0.15
7. Americans like to dominate other people	-1.43
8. Americans are a peaceful people.	-0.27
9. Many Americans engage in criminal activities.	-0.29
10. Americans are very concerned about their poor.	0.29
11. Americans have strong family values.	0.74
12. There is little for which I admire Americans.	-0.63
OVERALL AVERAGE	-0.83

-5 -4 -3 -2 -1 0 1 2 3 4 5
Negative　　Neutral　　Positive

Korea appears to present an example of Rudyard Kipling's principle. It was the United States that kept their country out of the communist sphere—with many thousands of American soldiers killed in the process. To understand what would have happened to their families and lives if that effort had not been made, one need only to look northward. It may seem to some that Kipling had it right. Helping, or even protecting, people can earn enmity and not gratitude—at least among many. Furthermore, events of the past are ephemeral and just dry history for subsequent generations and seem to have little carry-over to current attitudes, beliefs and opinions.

At the same time, many thousands of American troops have had a very visible presence in South Korea for more than half a century. Korean youths see American soldiers every day on the streets of Seoul and elsewhere. To them, it can appear that the United States is *occupying* their country. An analogy would be this: If British troops had come to the United States half a century ago to assist in repelling an invasion, and if many thousands of them remained for half a century, our teenagers might come to believe that Great Britain was occupying their country.

If the views of teenagers studied in South Korea seem difficult to explain, those of Mexico are even more so. There are no U.S. troops there. But, clearly, ordinary Americans are not held in high regard by the young people studied. They were more negative than those in the People's Republic of China—with which we have long had significant differences. Mexico was also more negative than the Muslim country of Pakistan. Obviously, other factors are at work here.

Somewhat the same comment can be made about Taiwan. The teenagers studied in Beijing were more favorable toward Americans than those in Taipei. The American government is spending vast sums to protect that island population from the demands of The People's Republic of China. If it were not for that protection, the people of Taiwan would be leading the more regimented life-style of a communist society.

Teenagers from Nigeria and Italy were not negative—merely neutral. Several factors could be playing a part in the case of Italy. It certainly has few Muslims. However, many American families came originally from Italy, and the United States played a key role liberating that country from fascism decades ago in World War II. Perhaps some vestige of those factors remain as a foundation for current beliefs and attitudes.

It is not easy to explain the neutral findings from Nigeria. The United States has not been particularly involved with that country on any sustained basis. Nigeria has been neither a source of extensive immigration to the United States, nor, particularly, a recipient of its assistance. With so little involvement, it appears that Kipling's principle does not apply.

Argentina was the only country of the twelve in which teenagers generally gave Americans positive marks. This finding is truly difficult to understand. The United States has not played a particularly positive role in Argentine affairs. Indeed the United States sided with the British when Argentina attempted to claim the Faulkland Islands by military force in 1982. However, that does not seem to have provided a basis for teenage negative views of Americans. It may be that the limited U.S. involvement in the affairs of Argentina is the foundation of the respondents' positive attitudes—compared to, say, Mexico, with which we are closely involved.

The reasons for teenagers' negative views of Americans in some of the countries are not difficult to understand. The religious factor undoubtedly plays a part in some. The influence of parents and other adults on the next generation also seems likely in some cases. Yet, in countries like South Korea, Mexico and Taiwan, the finding that young people hold negative beliefs about Americans is more difficult to explain.

PROFILES OF SPECIFIC BELIEFS ABOUT
AMERICANS OBTAINED IN EACH COUNTRY

Figures 1 and 2 provide overviews that combined the responses for each country. In contrast, Figures 3 through 14 on the pages that follow provide much greater detail. These twelve charts show how the subjects in each country responded to each of the evaluative statements in the attitude scale. Thus, they provide a detailed profile of how Americans are judged by the teenagers in the study.

A feature of these charts that stands out is their many differences. Some are obviously more negative on some statements than others, but in some, the respondents gave positive responses. Thus, no two are alike. This is an important finding in that no assumption can be made that overall assessments of attitudes (such as those shown earlier in Figures 1 and 2) can adequately describe the more subtle dimensions of positive or negative views of those who responded to the scale in a particular country.

RESPONSES BY EACH COUNTRY TO EACH ATTITUDE STATEMENT

The results obtained from each of the twelve attitude scale items, *considered one-by-one*, are shown in Figures 15 through 26 on the pages that follow. These twelve charts show the degree to which the respondents in each of the countries expressed positive or negative feelings about the particular statement shown at the top. On each chart, the countries are listed on the left *in rank order*—with the most negative country (for that statement) at the top and the most positive at the bottom.

As can be seen by examining these charts individually, there are numerous differences in the patterns of response to these statements of beliefs about Americans. As might be expected, Saudi-Arabia and Bahrain led in negative responses, reflecting their overall patterns as discussed in the previous section (Figures 1 and 2).

What was not evident in those charts was the *pattern* of positive and negative responses to the various statements for each country independently indicating beliefs about Americans. As might be anticipated, the subjects in the more favorable countries overall—namely Argentina and Nigeria—gave positive responses to many of the items. However, as was noted in the discussion of patterns in Figures 3 through14, countries that were negative in an overall sense—namely Pakistan, China and Taiwan—also gave positive responses to at least some of the individual statements.

Figure 3
Saudi Arabia: Beliefs About Americans (N=93)

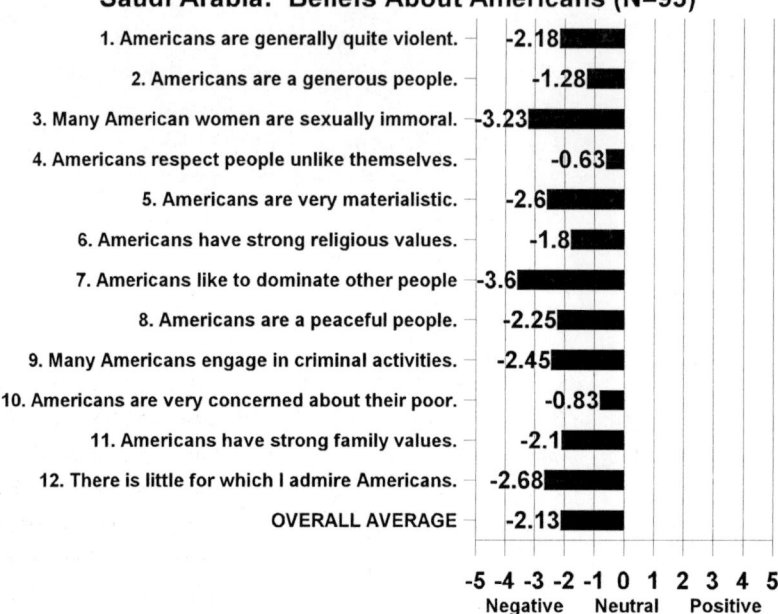

1. Americans are generally quite violent. — -2.18
2. Americans are a generous people. — -1.28
3. Many American women are sexually immoral. — -3.23
4. Americans respect people unlike themselves. — -0.63
5. Americans are very materialistic. — -2.6
6. Americans have strong religious values. — -1.8
7. Americans like to dominate other people — -3.6
8. Americans are a peaceful people. — -2.25
9. Many Americans engage in criminal activities. — -2.45
10. Americans are very concerned about their poor. — -0.83
11. Americans have strong family values. — -2.1
12. There is little for which I admire Americans. — -2.68
OVERALL AVERAGE — -2.13

-5 -4 -3 -2 -1 0 1 2 3 4 5
Negative   Neutral   Positive

Figure 4
Bahrain: Beliefs About Americans (N=100)

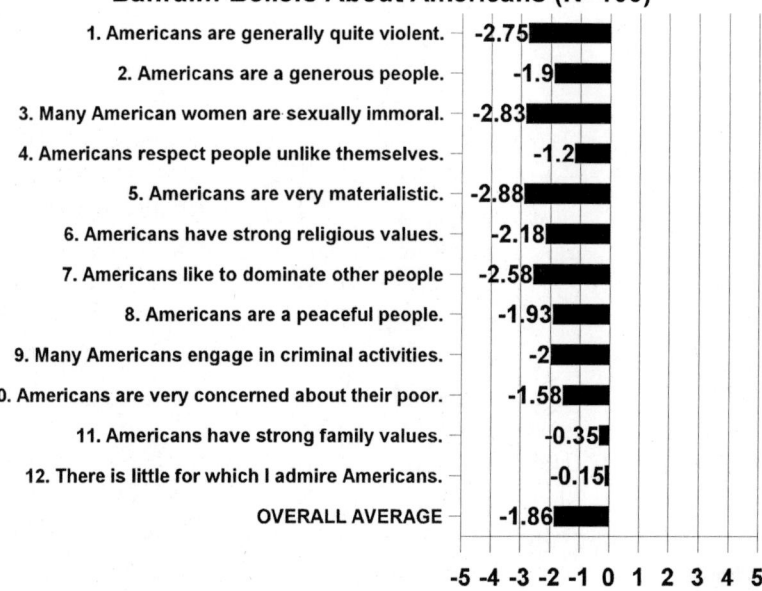

1. Americans are generally quite violent. — -2.75
2. Americans are a generous people. — -1.9
3. Many American women are sexually immoral. — -2.83
4. Americans respect people unlike themselves. — -1.2
5. Americans are very materialistic. — -2.88
6. Americans have strong religious values. — -2.18
7. Americans like to dominate other people — -2.58
8. Americans are a peaceful people. — -1.93
9. Many Americans engage in criminal activities. — -2
10. Americans are very concerned about their poor. — -1.58
11. Americans have strong family values. — -0.35
12. There is little for which I admire Americans. — -0.15
OVERALL AVERAGE — -1.86

-5 -4 -3 -2 -1 0 1 2 3 4 5
Negative   Neutral   Positive

Figure 5
South Korea: Beliefs About Americans (N=175)

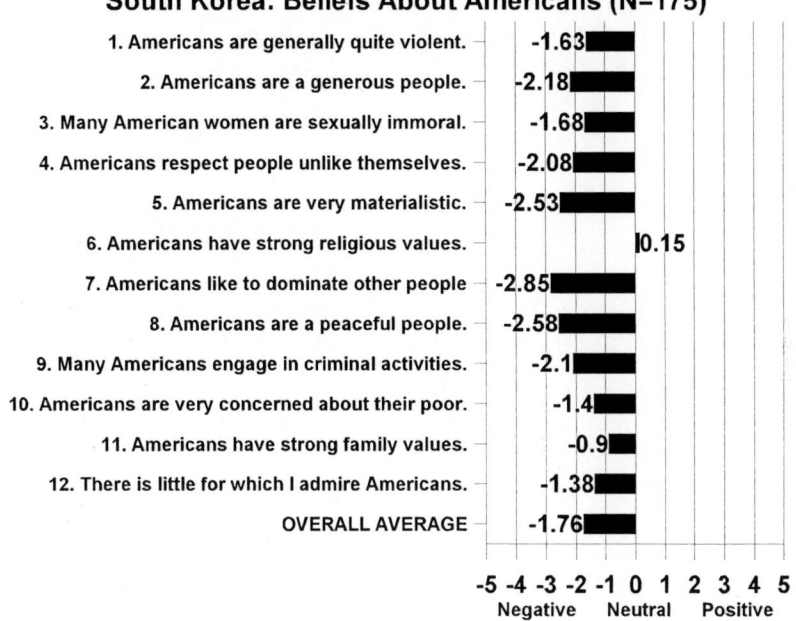

1. Americans are generally quite violent. — -1.63
2. Americans are a generous people. — -2.18
3. Many American women are sexually immoral. — -1.68
4. Americans respect people unlike themselves. — -2.08
5. Americans are very materialistic. — -2.53
6. Americans have strong religious values. — 0.15
7. Americans like to dominate other people — -2.85
8. Americans are a peaceful people. — -2.58
9. Many Americans engage in criminal activities. — -2.1
10. Americans are very concerned about their poor. — -1.4
11. Americans have strong family values. — -0.9
12. There is little for which I admire Americans. — -1.38
OVERALL AVERAGE — -1.76

-5 -4 -3 -2 -1 0 1 2 3 4 5
Negative   Neutral   Positive

Figure 6
Lebanon: Beliefs About Americans (N=103)

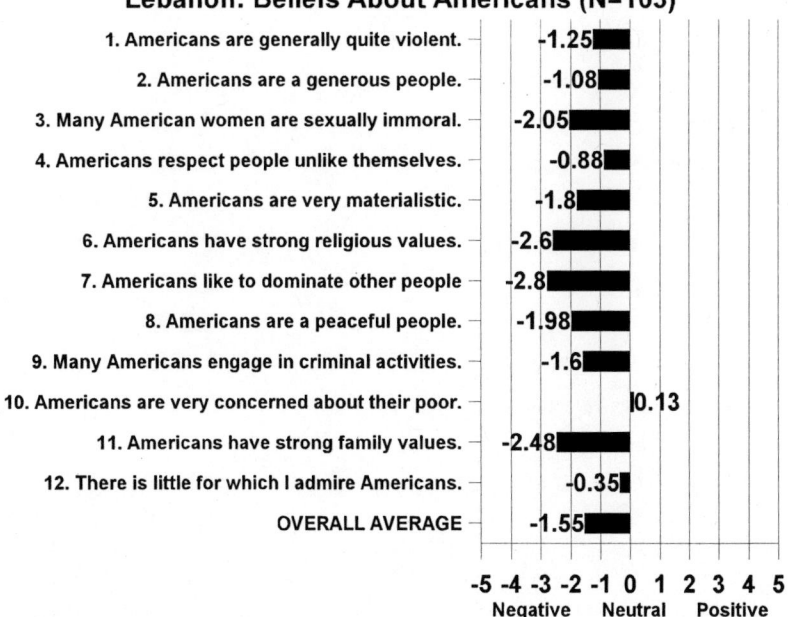

1. Americans are generally quite violent. — -1.25
2. Americans are a generous people. — -1.08
3. Many American women are sexually immoral. — -2.05
4. Americans respect people unlike themselves. — -0.88
5. Americans are very materialistic. — -1.8
6. Americans have strong religious values. — -2.6
7. Americans like to dominate other people — -2.8
8. Americans are a peaceful people. — -1.98
9. Many Americans engage in criminal activities. — -1.6
10. Americans are very concerned about their poor. — 0.13
11. Americans have strong family values. — -2.48
12. There is little for which I admire Americans. — -0.35
OVERALL AVERAGE — -1.55

-5 -4 -3 -2 -1 0 1 2 3 4 5
Negative   Neutral   Positive

Figure 7
Mexico: Beliefs About Americans (N=128)

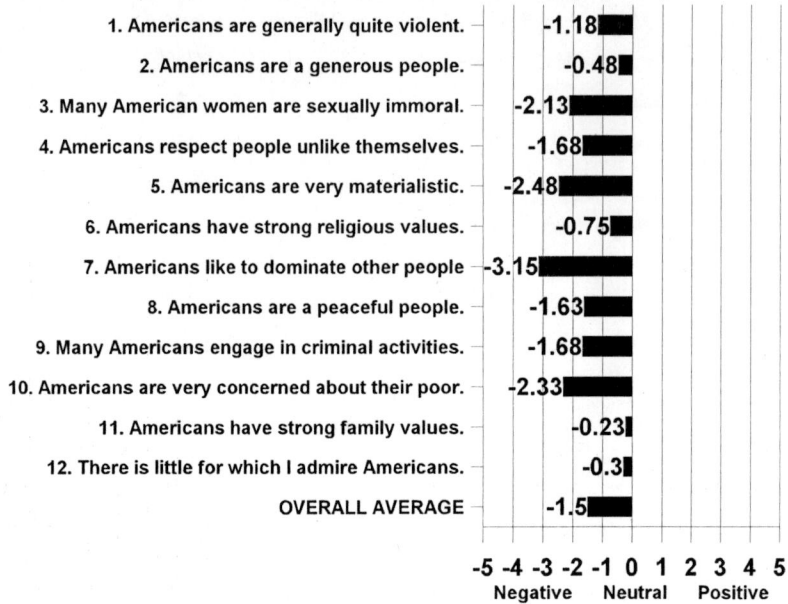

Figure 8
China: Beliefs About Americans (N=99)

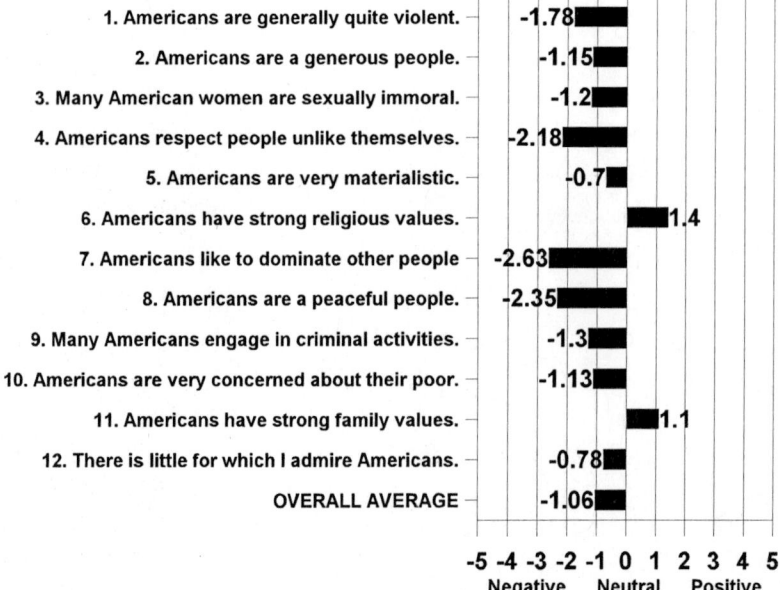

Figure 9

Spain: Beliefs About Americans (N=109)

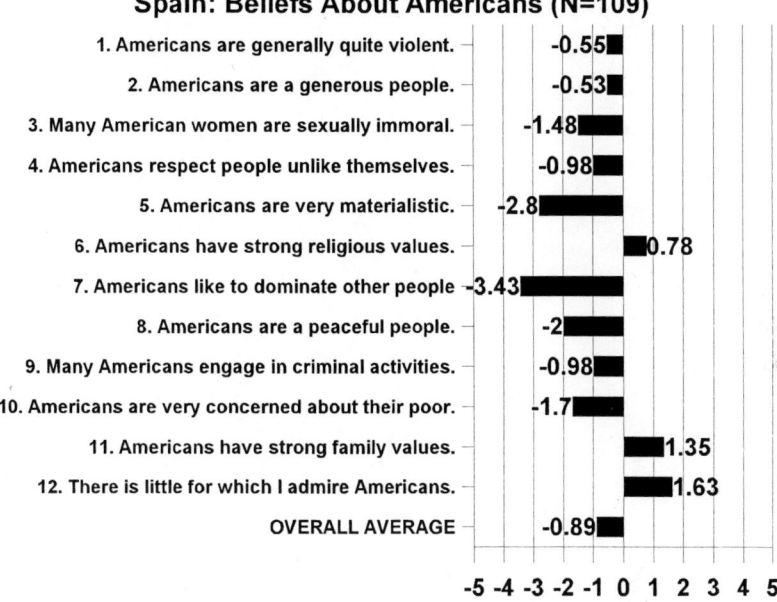

Figure 10

Taiwan: Beliefs About Americans (N=101)

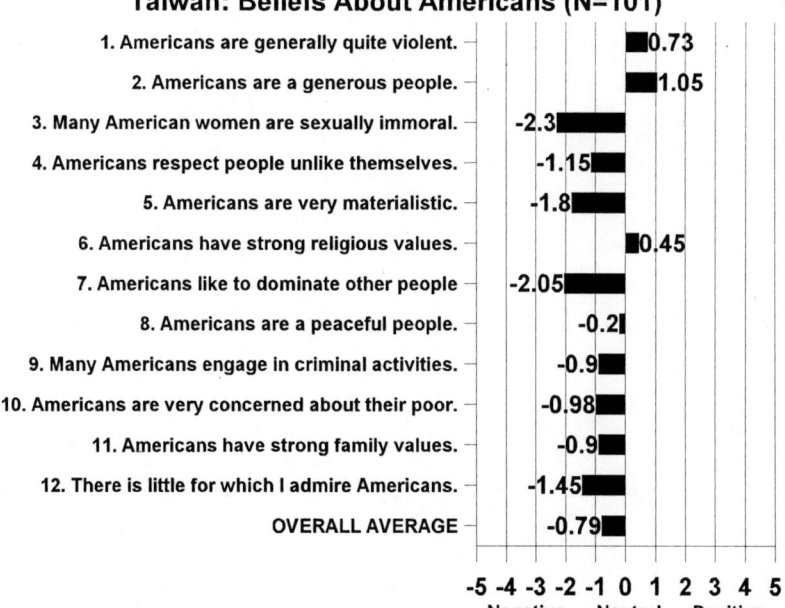

Figure 11
Pakistan: Beliefs About Americans (N=139)

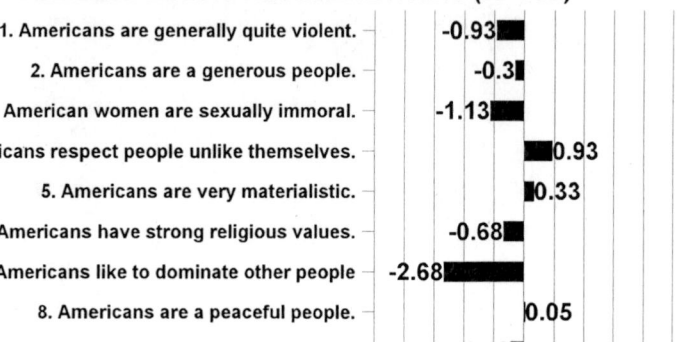

1. Americans are generally quite violent.	-0.93
2. Americans are a generous people.	-0.3
3. Many American women are sexually immoral.	-1.13
4. Americans respect people unlike themselves.	0.93
5. Americans are very materialistic.	0.33
6. Americans have strong religious values.	-0.68
7. Americans like to dominate other people	-2.68
8. Americans are a peaceful people.	0.05
9. Many Americans engage in criminal activities.	-0.43
10. Americans are very concerned about their poor.	0.3
11. Americans have strong family values.	-0.83
12. There is little for which I admire Americans.	-0.18
OVERALL AVERAGE	-0.46

-5 -4 -3 -2 -1 0 1 2 3 4 5
Negative   Neutral   Positive

Figure 12
Nigeria: Beliefs About Americans (N=97)

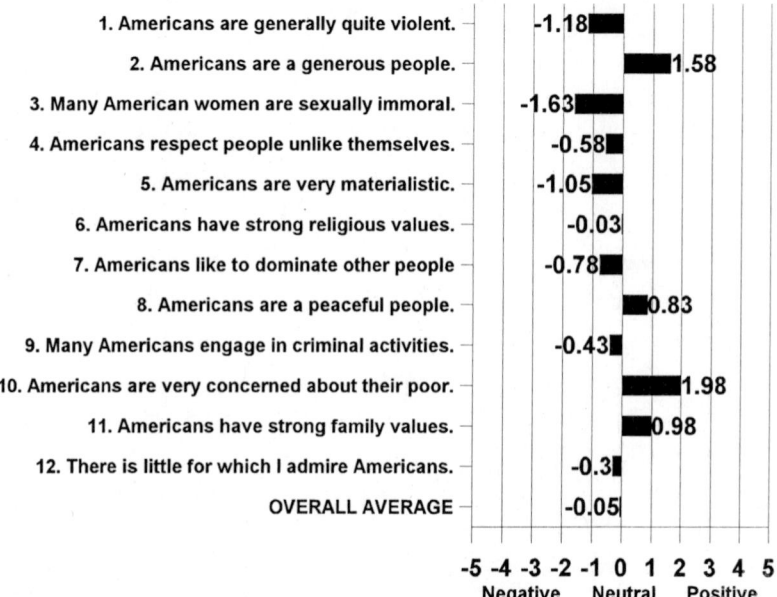

1. Americans are generally quite violent.	-1.18
2. Americans are a generous people.	1.58
3. Many American women are sexually immoral.	-1.63
4. Americans respect people unlike themselves.	-0.58
5. Americans are very materialistic.	-1.05
6. Americans have strong religious values.	-0.03
7. Americans like to dominate other people	-0.78
8. Americans are a peaceful people.	0.83
9. Many Americans engage in criminal activities.	-0.43
10. Americans are very concerned about their poor.	1.98
11. Americans have strong family values.	0.98
12. There is little for which I admire Americans.	-0.3
OVERALL AVERAGE	-0.05

-5 -4 -3 -2 -1 0 1 2 3 4 5
Negative   Neutral   Positive

Figure 13
Italy: Beliefs About Americans (N=82)

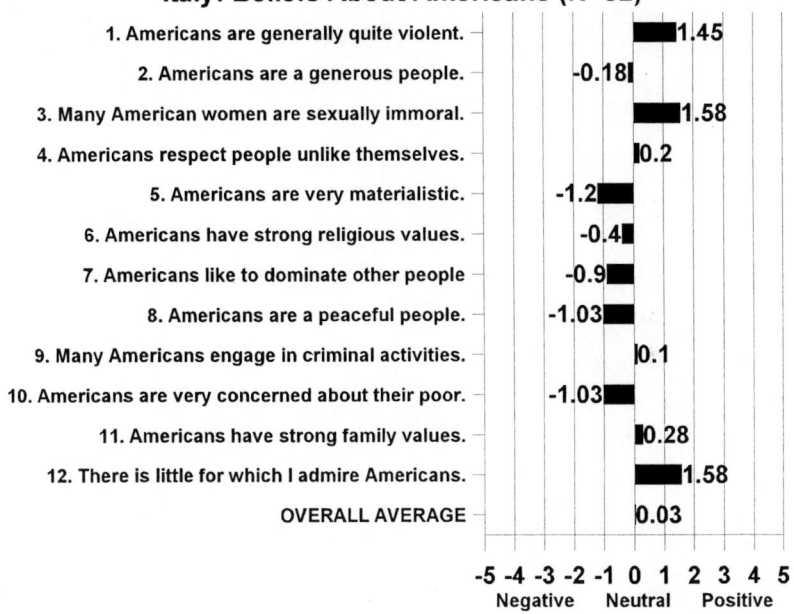

1. Americans are generally quite violent. — 1.45
2. Americans are a generous people. — -0.18
3. Many American women are sexually immoral. — 1.58
4. Americans respect people unlike themselves. — 0.2
5. Americans are very materialistic. — -1.2
6. Americans have strong religious values. — -0.4
7. Americans like to dominate other people — -0.9
8. Americans are a peaceful people. — -1.03
9. Many Americans engage in criminal activities. — 0.1
10. Americans are very concerned about their poor. — -1.03
11. Americans have strong family values. — 0.28
12. There is little for which I admire Americans. — 1.58

OVERALL AVERAGE — 0.03

-5 -4 -3 -2 -1 0 1 2 3 4 5
Negative   Neutral   Positive

Figure 14
Argentina: Beliefs About Americans (N=105)

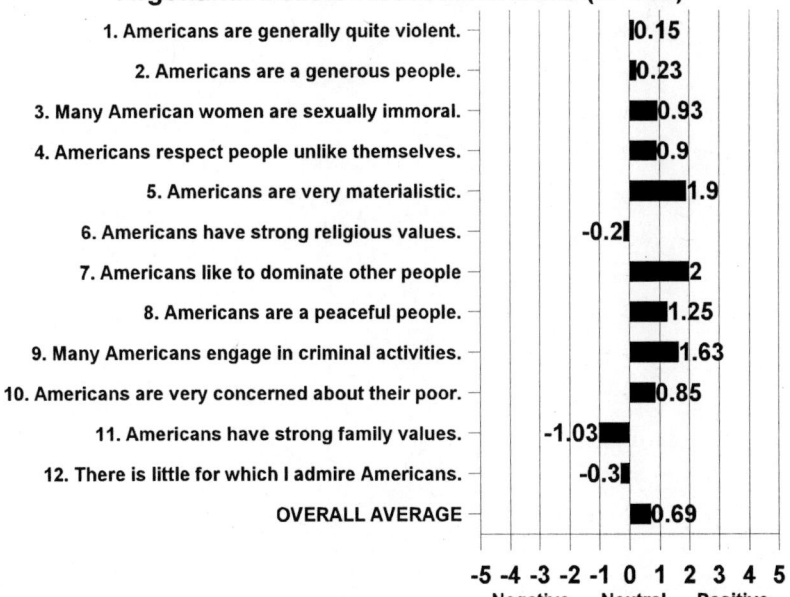

1. Americans are generally quite violent. — 0.15
2. Americans are a generous people. — 0.23
3. Many American women are sexually immoral. — 0.93
4. Americans respect people unlike themselves. — 0.9
5. Americans are very materialistic. — 1.9
6. Americans have strong religious values. — -0.2
7. Americans like to dominate other people — 2
8. Americans are a peaceful people. — 1.25
9. Many Americans engage in criminal activities. — 1.63
10. Americans are very concerned about their poor. — 0.85
11. Americans have strong family values. — -1.03
12. There is little for which I admire Americans. — -0.3

OVERALL AVERAGE — 0.69

-5 -4 -3 -2 -1 0 1 2 3 4 5
Negative   Neutral   Positive

Figure 15
"Americans Are Generally Quite Violent"

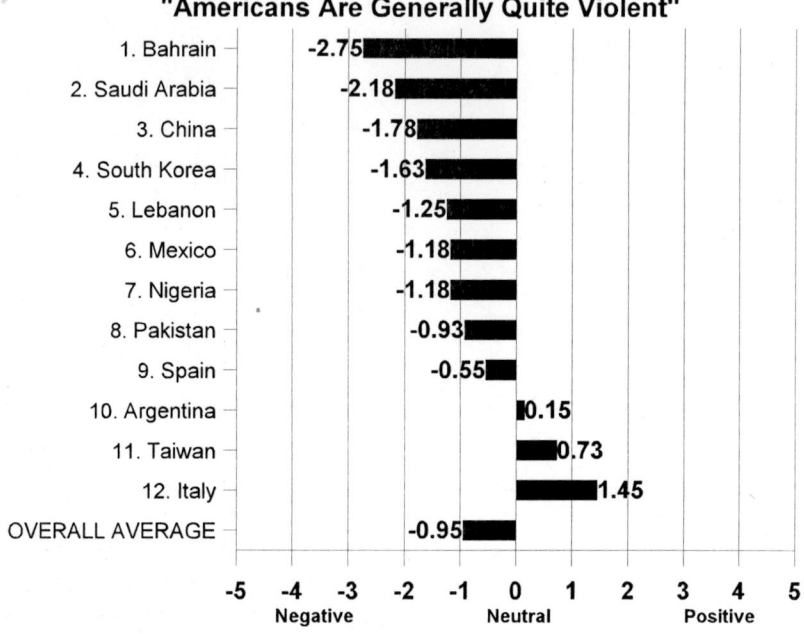

1. Bahrain	-2.75
2. Saudi Arabia	-2.18
3. China	-1.78
4. South Korea	-1.63
5. Lebanon	-1.25
6. Mexico	-1.18
7. Nigeria	-1.18
8. Pakistan	-0.93
9. Spain	-0.55
10. Argentina	0.15
11. Taiwan	0.73
12. Italy	1.45
OVERALL AVERAGE	-0.95

-5   -4   -3   -2   -1   0   1   2   3   4   5
Negative   Neutral   Positive

Figure 16
"Americans Are a Generous People"

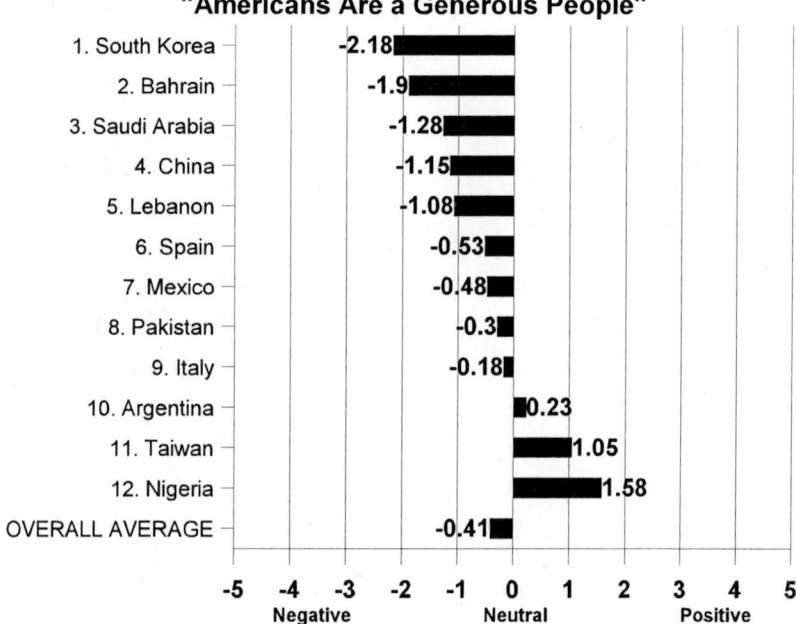

1. South Korea	-2.18
2. Bahrain	-1.9
3. Saudi Arabia	-1.28
4. China	-1.15
5. Lebanon	-1.08
6. Spain	-0.53
7. Mexico	-0.48
8. Pakistan	-0.3
9. Italy	-0.18
10. Argentina	0.23
11. Taiwan	1.05
12. Nigeria	1.58
OVERALL AVERAGE	-0.41

-5   -4   -3   -2   -1   0   1   2   3   4   5
Negative   Neutral   Positive

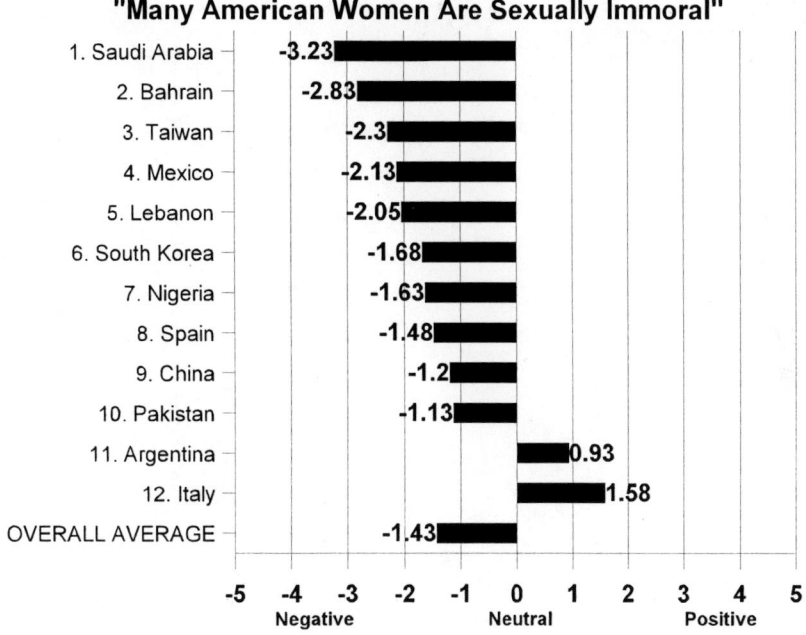

Figure 17

"Many American Women Are Sexually Immoral"

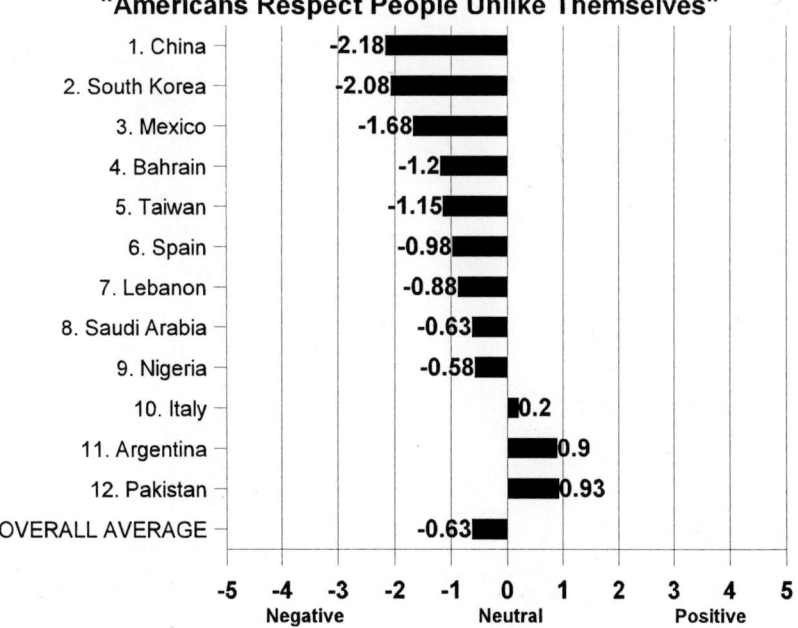

Figure 18

"Americans Respect People Unlike Themselves"

Figure 19
"Americans Are Very Materialistic"

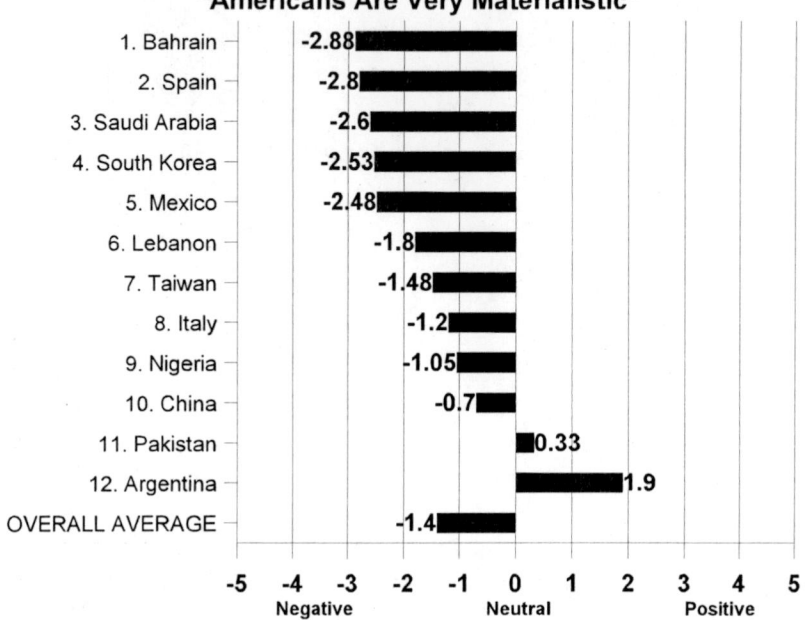

1. Bahrain	-2.88
2. Spain	-2.8
3. Saudi Arabia	-2.6
4. South Korea	-2.53
5. Mexico	-2.48
6. Lebanon	-1.8
7. Taiwan	-1.48
8. Italy	-1.2
9. Nigeria	-1.05
10. China	-0.7
11. Pakistan	0.33
12. Argentina	1.9
OVERALL AVERAGE	-1.4

-5 -4 -3 -2 -1 0 1 2 3 4 5
Negative   Neutral   Positive

Figure 20
"Americans Have Strong Religious Values"

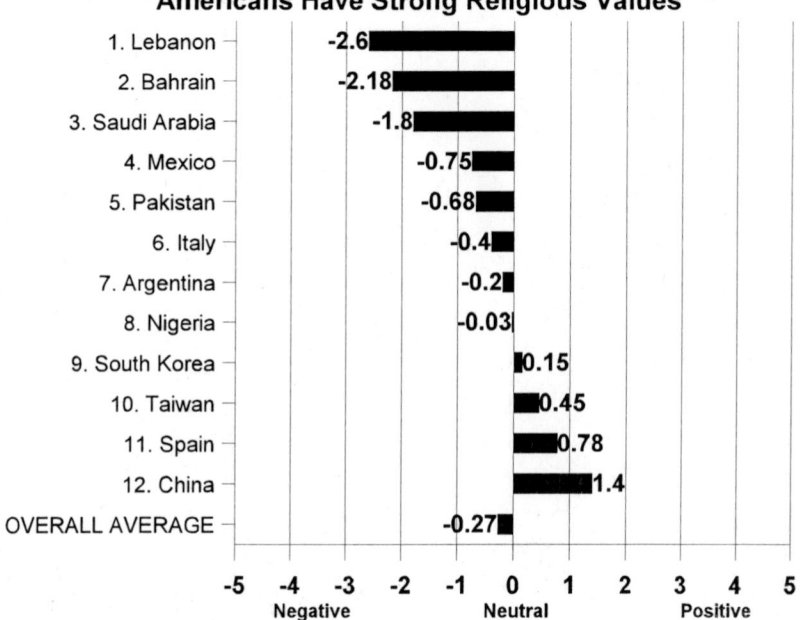

1. Lebanon	-2.6
2. Bahrain	-2.18
3. Saudi Arabia	-1.8
4. Mexico	-0.75
5. Pakistan	-0.68
6. Italy	-0.4
7. Argentina	-0.2
8. Nigeria	-0.03
9. South Korea	0.15
10. Taiwan	0.45
11. Spain	0.78
12. China	1.4
OVERALL AVERAGE	-0.27

-5 -4 -3 -2 -1 0 1 2 3 4 5
Negative   Neutral   Positive

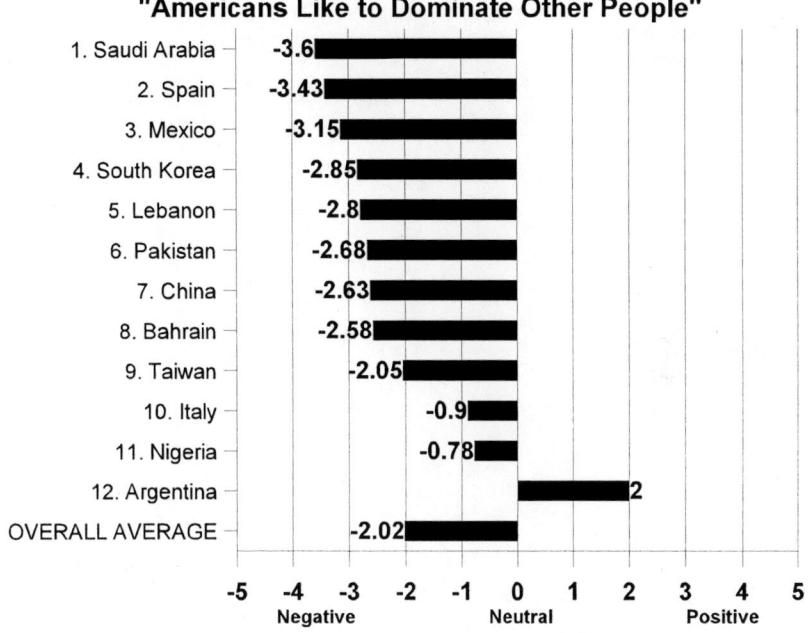

Figure 21
"Americans Like to Dominate Other People"

Figure 22
"Americans Are a Peaceful People"

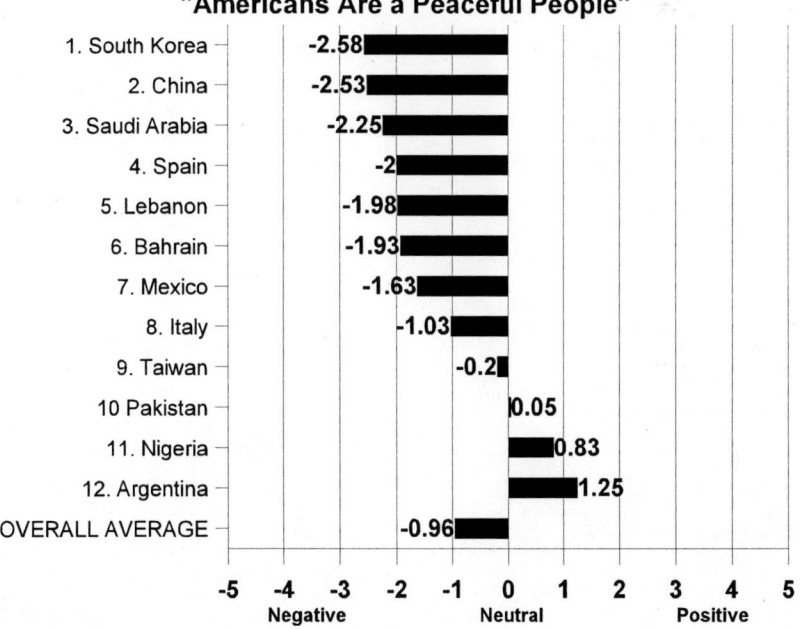

Figure 23
"Many Americans Engage in Criminal Activities"

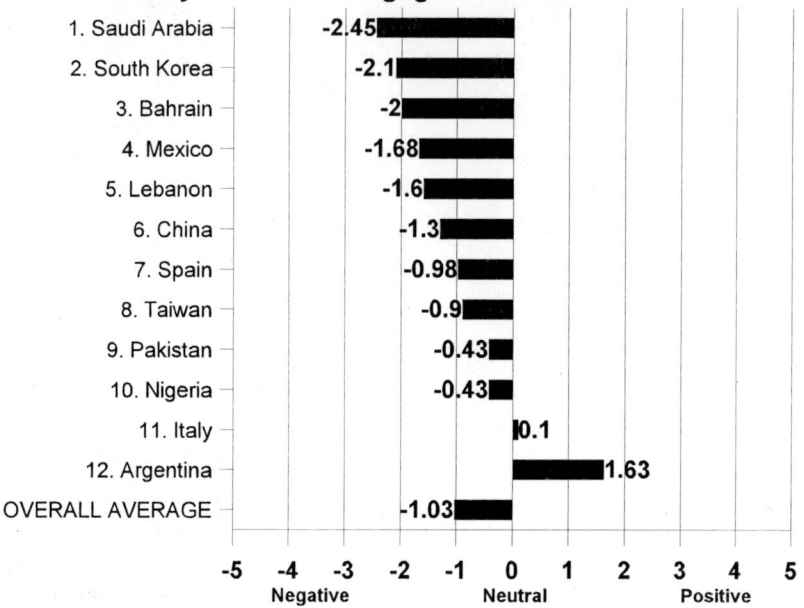

Figure 24
"Americans Are Very Concerned About Their Poor"

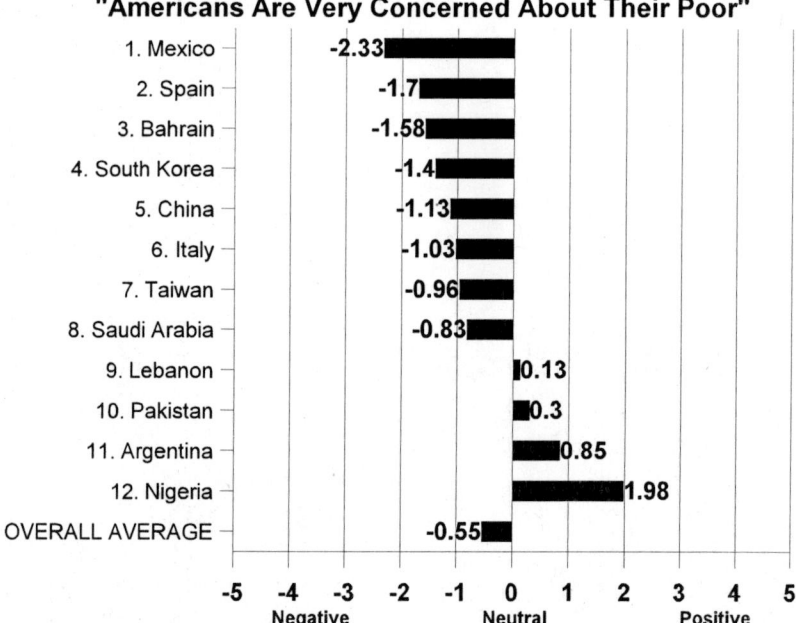

Figure 25
"Americans Have Strong Family Values"

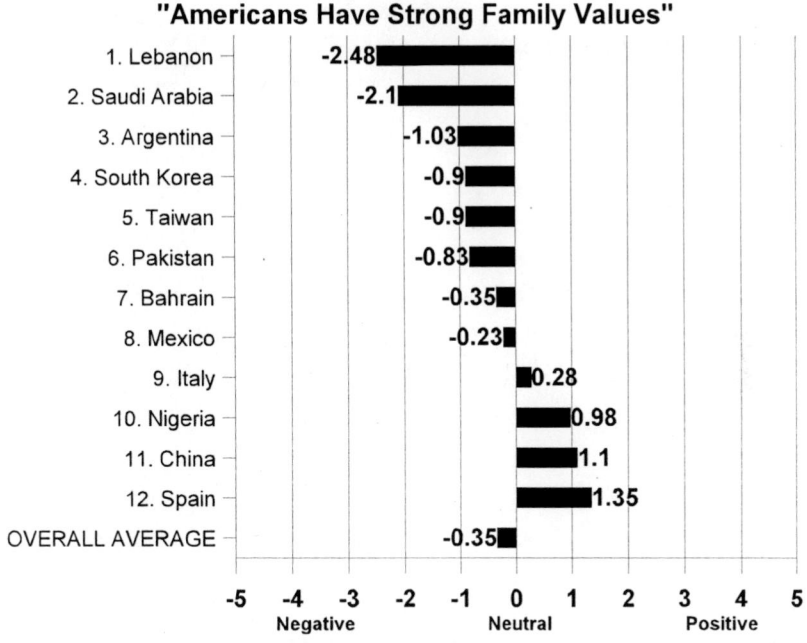

1. Lebanon — -2.48
2. Saudi Arabia — -2.1
3. Argentina — -1.03
4. South Korea — -0.9
5. Taiwan — -0.9
6. Pakistan — -0.83
7. Bahrain — -0.35
8. Mexico — -0.23
9. Italy — 0.28
10. Nigeria — 0.98
11. China — 1.1
12. Spain — 1.35
OVERALL AVERAGE — -0.35

-5 -4 -3 -2 -1 0 1 2 3 4 5
Negative   Neutral   Positive

Figure 26
"There is Little for Which I Admire Americans"

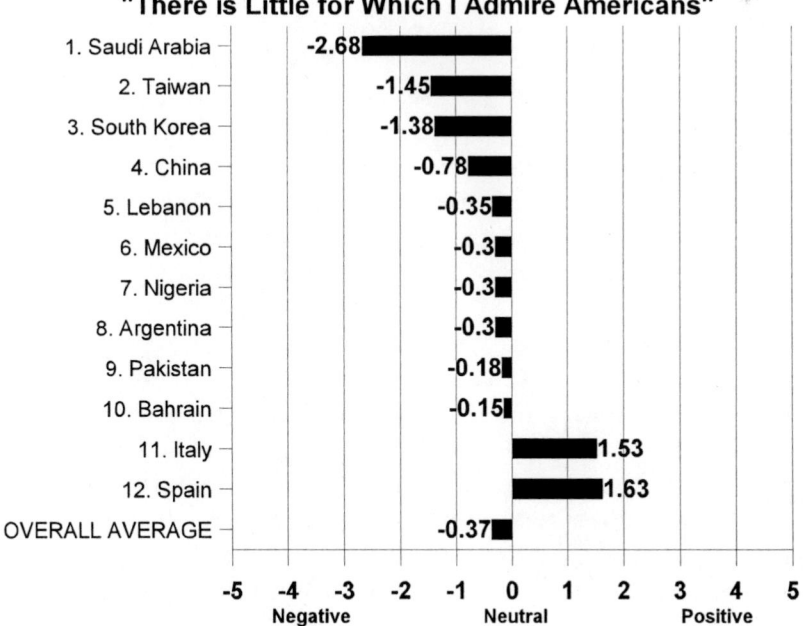

1. Saudi Arabia — -2.68
2. Taiwan — -1.45
3. South Korea — -1.38
4. China — -0.78
5. Lebanon — -0.35
6. Mexico — -0.3
7. Nigeria — -0.3
8. Argentina — -0.3
9. Pakistan — -0.18
10. Bahrain — -0.15
11. Italy — 1.53
12. Spain — 1.63
OVERALL AVERAGE — -0.37

-5 -4 -3 -2 -1 0 1 2 3 4 5
Negative   Neutral   Positive

Absent from this positive category is Mexico. Even though the young respondents from Mexico were not the most negative toward Americans in an overall sense (Figure 1), there was no single item in the Likert Scale to which, on average, they gave a positive response. Even the teenagers in Pakistan and China gave positive responses to at least two of the items.

Again, what is important about Figures 15 through 26 is the very different patterns of responses that were found in the twelve countries concerning each of the twelve specific statements of evaluative beliefs. What this implies, once more, is that measuring how people feel about Americans is by no means *unidimensional.* Respondents, such as the youths studied in the present project, are not *uniformly* positive or negative on every dimension of their attitudes. One size does not fit all.

This finding is consistent with the basic definition of attitude stated earlier—as a set of evaluative beliefs toward an object. Some beliefs are more, and some less, negative. Others can be more, or less, positive. This fact concerning the nature of evaluative beliefs concerning an attitude object can be important information for designing a strategy to change the attitudes of a set of respondents toward that attitude object.

RESULTS OBTAINED FROM THE MEDIA INFLUENCES SUBSCALE

As explained, the attitude scale administered to the respondents included three items that can be combined to produce a *Media Influences Subscale.* It was designed to show the influences of images of Americans *derived from their depictions in media entertainment products and popular culture, such as movies and television programming.* In many ways, the findings obtained with this subscale are the most important in the entire project. The purpose in developing this goal was to try and understand the *sources* of the flawed and negative images of ordinary Americans that are shown in the 26 charts already presented.

The specific items making up the subscale are these:

> *Item 1:* "Americans are generally quite violent."
> *Item 3:* "American women are sexually immoral."
> *Item 9:* "Many Americans engage in criminal activities."

Why were these particular items selected as indicators of how Americans are depicted in media entertainment products? The reason, suggested earlier, is simply this: Violence, sex and crime are the most common themes that producers of such media content use to attract the attention of and provide gratification for their youthful audiences. Anyone who doubts that has only to go to a recent movie, view a serial drama on television, play a computer game or listen to the lyrics of the latest popular song. These are the themes that have long been used to increase audience size. They have also been the subject of complaints by many critics of the media.

It can be noted as a side issue (not specifically studied in this project) that, in many ways, the *news media* also have long been aware of and dependent on the use of these same themes—both domestically and internationally—to enhance interest in their product, which maximizes audience and profits. In their use of "news values" to select the stories that will make up the agenda of the daily newspaper or broadcast, editors and news directors are very likely to include stories about violent acts, crime and sexually titillating events. Like other media, this pattern of selection is a product of their competitive situation and their need to maximize their audiences in order to increase profits.

In recent times, such stories have dominated the daily news agenda. They have included numerous reports of shootings at schools, unethical and illegal dealings by business executives, homosexual exploitation of young boys by religious leaders and sexual misconduct with young women by military leaders and politicians in high offices. To a young person in a conservative country who keeps up with the news from the United States, these depictions can appear to offer important insights about the behavior and moral nature of Americans. As noted, however, the content and influence of the news media are not a central focus of the present project.

The results obtained from the subscale are shown in Figure 27 and in Table 2. The table (see page 73) presents the results of a statistical analysis based on the concept of *correlation*. Readers who are familiar with this statistical procedure need no explanation of its nature and uses. However, for those unfamiliar with this idea, it is not difficult to understand. A correlation coefficient is an index that expresses in a single number the relationship that exists between two columns of figures, both of which represent observations made on some set of individuals.

For example, imagine a large number of persons—a hundred or so—whose height and weight has been measured and recorded. Since tall people tend to be heavier than short people, one would expect these twin sets of numbers to correspond in some way. They would "co-vary" or be "co-related" in the sense that a large number in the height column for a person would have a corresponding large number in the weight column. The same type of co-relationship would be the case for short people. There would be smaller numbers in both columns.

This kind of relationship between such numbers in two columns can be

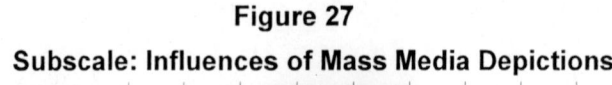

Figure 27
Subscale: Influences of Mass Media Depictions

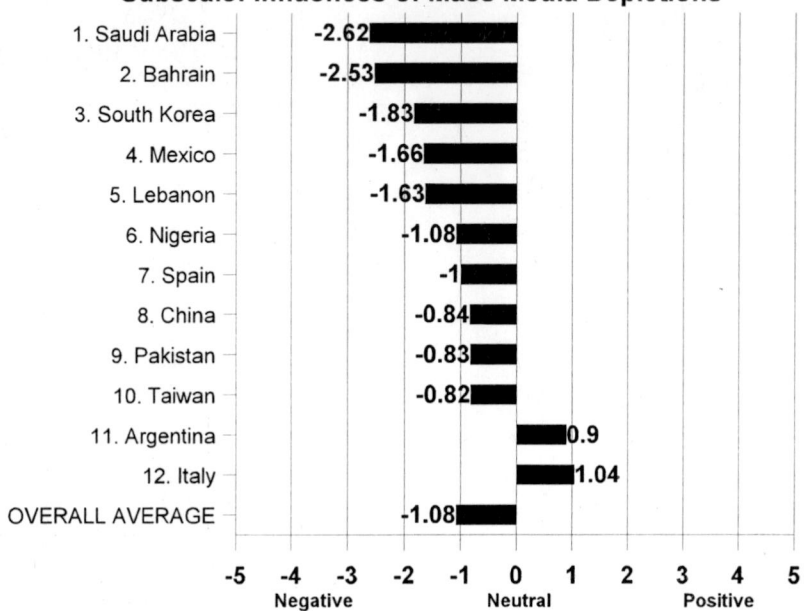

expressed mathematically by calculating a "correlation coefficient." If the numbers are perfectly matched in this co-variation sense, that coefficient would have a maximum value of +1.0. Every large or small number in the first column would have a counterpart of the same relative magnitude in the second—a high correlation indeed.

Such large values are almost never found in nature. On the other hand if the numbers the two columns just varied randomly—with no co-variation at all—the calculated coefficient of correlation would be *zero*. In most such comparisons that are calculated from observations made on people, the value of the coefficient is somewhere in between those extremes. (We can add that there is also the case that when one number is small the other is large—a situation that is called "negative correlation." That too can range between zero and one—minus one in this case—but that situation need not concern us here.)

The actual correlation coefficients found with the use of the Media Influences Subscale can be seen in Table 2 on the next page, but they require additional explanation in order to interpret what they mean for the objectives of the present project.

TABLE 2
CORRELATIONS BETWEEN THE
MEDIA INFLUENCES SUBSCALE AND THE ATTITUDE SCALE

Subscale Item	Americans Are Violent	American Women Are Immoral	Americans Are Criminals	Media Influences Subscale	Attitude Scale
1. Americans Are Violent	-----				.423*
3. American Women Are Immoral		-----			.288*
9. Americans Are Criminals			-----		.443*
Media Influences Subscale				-----	.527*
N=1,313 *Significance level <.0001					

Note that the Attitude Scale scores (far right column) were calculated as the *mean* (that is, average) score earned by the subjects on the nine items that are not part of the Media Influences Subscale. Recall also that the values for each subject on the Media Influences Subscale represent the *mean* (average) scores earned by each subject on those three items. Thus, the two measures are *independent* when calculated in this form and there is no concern that they are measures of the same thing. For that reason, a correlation coefficient between the subscale and the attitude measure can be calculated to show the degree to which they co-vary together. As can be seen, the value of that coefficient is +.527.

Table 2 also shows the correlation coefficients between each of the three items that make up the Media Subscale and the revised Attitude Scale score (as indicated at the right in Table 2). These have some significance as indicators of the contribution of each of the three to the relationship between the Media Subscale and the Attitude Scale. Of much greater importance, however, is the correlation coefficient (+.527) in the lower right corner, indicating the relationship between the (three-item) *Media Influences Subscale* and the *Attitude Scale* (based on the remaining nine items).

Note that the starred footnote (located below the table) to the values in the right hand column indicates the "significance level" of each of the starred correlation coefficients. This is important information. What it indicates for each starred coefficient is the *probability* that this particular value could have *simply occurred by chance*. What does that mean? Imagine that a huge army of many thousands of subjects had randomly responded to the various items and subscales, selecting their responses not on the basis of what they believed or felt, but totally by chance. How likely would it be, under those circumstances, that the starred correlation coefficients would have the values shown?

The fact is that the probability that a correlation coefficient of + .527 (or any of those listed) could be a result of that kind of random process is virtually zero. How do we know that? The answer is that such probabilities are sensitive to the *numbers of subjects* involved in the calculation. The larger the number, the more "reliable" (less chance-like) the results. In this case, that number is 1,313 subjects—which is a very large number from which to calculate a correlation coefficient. Indeed, the probability that these results (coefficients this large) could represent mere chance-like events is so remote that it could not even be calculated to more than 17 decimal places by the computer software used to try and determine it.

What is the "bottom line" here? What do all of these correlation coefficients, subscales and significance values mean with respect to the overall objectives of the present project? Essentially, they mean that the young people studied have been significantly influenced by depictions of Americans as violent, as criminally inclined and women in the United States as sexually immoral. There is simply *no way that these correlations can be dismissed as chance-like*. With 1,313 sets of observations, the items included in the Media Influences Subscale are overwhelmingly co-related with the values for the subjects on the Attitude Scale.

But there is a second issue that must be addressed. Because two columns of figures are correlated, does that mean that one *causes* the other? This is a very complex question, but the answer is sometimes "yes," but sometimes "no!" It all depends on what the numbers refer to. In some cases, a causal relationship is intuitively evident with little doubt. On the other hand, sometimes it is intuitively evident that no such causal relationship could possibly exist. At still other times, the correlation between the two columns may be an artifact, with the numbers in each being caused by still a third factor.

It is important to confront this issue in the present project. It is after all, an attempt to identify the sources from which young people in a dozen societies have put together their views of Americans. Has the content of what they view that depicts Americans in media entertainment (violence, sex, and criminal behavior) played any kind of causal role in producing their (largely negative) views?

Examples will aid in understanding the conclusions reached on this issue.

Imagine the following situation: A list of persons has been obtained who died of lung cancer. Information is available of how many cigarettes on average each smoked on a daily basis, as well as the number of years that each lived. The question is this: Are these sets of numbers co-related? And if so, does one serve as a cause for the other? It does not take the proverbial "rocket scientist" to reach the conclusion that the cigarettes were a causal factor in the deaths. It would be absurd to go the other way and say that the number of years they lived before death had caused the number of smokes that each person had enjoyed on a daily basis.

But let us consider a different case. This is a traditional one often used by statisticians to explain that what *appears* to be a causal relationship may not be so at all—and that a high correlation may actually be due to a third factor. To illustrate the ideas we can use two sets of measures obtained in Holland years ago. In the various counties in that country, the *birth rate* (number of babies born per woman) was found to be highly correlated with the number of *storks* present in the county. Draw your own conclusions about a causal inference! On closer examination, it was realized that birth rates tend to be higher in rural counties (among farm families) than they are in urban counties (where families are smaller). In addition, there are also more storks in rural counties than in urban ones. Thus, the correlation between birth rates and storks was an *artifact*. It was the rural vs urban nature of the county that was producing the effect.

These problems of interpretation need to be considered in the case of the (high) correlation found between the Media Subscale and the Attitude Scale. Do we have a stork problem here? Perhaps the negative attitudes toward Americans found among many of the youths studied merely reflect the views of their parents. They may have been taught that the United States is an object toward which one should have pejorative feelings. Such beliefs may have been encouraged in their schools or perhaps by their religious leaders. It is no secret that in some of the Muslim fundamentalist schools, students are taught that the United States is a Great Satan, and that non-believers (like Americans) are the *infidel*.

However, it is difficult to imagine that such sources would deliberately teach young people that American women are sexually immoral, that as human beings, Americans are violent and are criminally inclined. A more likely source for such beliefs is what young audiences acquire (through incidental learning) from media entertainment products that depict ordinary Americans in these ways.

To sort out the question of the part played by religion, one needs to turn to the charts of results presented earlier. While it is clear that the two countries where youths have the most negative beliefs and attitudes toward Americans have

Muslim populations (Saudi Arabia and Bahrain. See Figure 1), *others with negative beliefs do not*. Neither South Korea, Mexico, China, Spain nor Taiwan have significant numbers of Muslims. There are simply no systematic lessons taught by *mullahs* in those countries defining Americans as infidels.

However, the youths studied in those countries clearly do have, to one degree or another, negative views of Americans. The religious factor, then, may play a part in a limited number of countries, but it is certainly not an important causal factor in most. In addition, there is little reason to believe that in the high schools attended by youths in any of those countries there is a systematic effort to teach negative beliefs and attitudes about ordinary people who live in the United States. What is left, then, is the influence of what young people learn when they go to the media to be entertained.

Stated in simple terms, therefore, the conclusion that emerges from the analysis of the Media Influences Subscale is this: The depiction of Americans in media content as *violent*, of American women as *sexually immoral* and of many Americans engaging in *criminal acts* has brought many of these 1,313 youthful subjects to hold generally negative attitudes toward people who live in the United States. The correlations and their significance values leave no other reasonable interpretation. Is it possible that these 1,313 youths formed their negative views of Americans in some other unknown way—other than learning about them from popular culture and media entertainment? Perhaps. But the present results appear to indicate that it is likely indeed that the entertainment content produced in Hollywood and other production centers of popular culture has influenced those studied in ways harmful to Americans.

In summary, the results presented in Figures 1 through 27, as well as in Table 2, show that the teenage respondents in nearly all of the countries studied held negative attitudes toward ordinary Americans. Only teenagers in Argentina were generally positive. The profiles of evaluative beliefs about Americans described by the twelve statements in the scale varied considerably from country-to-country—indicating that the dimensions and bases for negative attitudes were by no means the same in each. Negative mass media depictions of Americans in movies and TV programs appeared to have influenced the beliefs of many of the subjects—with other possible influences from factors not addressed in the present project.

There is an additional and important issue that must be addressed: While the various results presented show the *end product*—the consequences that occur when millions of young people in various societies around the world turn to media content and popular culture for entertainment and gratification—those results do not explain the *process*. That is, *why* do producers of such content develop it the way they do? *Why* do young people find popular culture produced mainly in the United States so attractive? *What* are the subtle lessons about Americans that are embedded in that media content? And *how* is it that they help form the impressions on Americans that have been described?

The next chapter will address these questions in detail by developing a multi-stage explanation of the process by which these events and consequences occur. It will review a formal explanation of each stage in the process, one at a time, and then integrate them into multi-stage or "master" theory.

CHAPTER ENDNOTES

1. See: "Viewpoints," *Newsday*, March 22, 2002, p. A35.

CHAPTER 6

A MULTI-STAGE EXPLANATION
OF MEDIA INFLUENCES

The results of this project can be interpreted within a perspective that includes a multi-stage explanation of background events, audience behavior and consequent media influences on young audiences around the world.

What this multi-stage explanatory sequence does is to bring together and *integrate* the following: (1) a theory concerning the *economic conditions* and requirements present in a capitalistic system within which the suppliers of media content operate, (2) a second theory explaining the *production strategies* that those suppliers use to meet those requirements, (3) theories explaining the *motivations and activities of audiences* that attend to the content that they produce, and finally, (4) additional theories explaining *how the consequences occur* that take place among those audiences—consequences that result from the attention that they give to the media products distributed by the producers.[1] In a real sense, therefore, what is being developed is a "master theory." It is an integrated explanation that may help us understand at least a major part of the question, "Why do they hate us?"

Bringing together a set of separate theories into one overall formulation is a step that is rarely taken by mass communication scholars. However, theory development in this field has progressed to the point where it is realistic to undertake such a task. The goal, then, is to bring together a set of more specific and narrowly focused theories (that now exist) into a more comprehensive explanation that provides an understanding of the several stages in the production, distribution of media content and its influences on audiences.

As explained below, the first step in trying to achieve that goal is to describe the fundamentals of the political and economic environment within which organizations that design, develop and distribute media content to a global audience must operate. It is important to realize that this environment has been *imposed upon them*. They did not invent it for their convenience. If they fail to meet the requirements of that economic system, they will fail to survive financially. There are few moral choices here. It is, in other words, a set of *prerequisites* for being successful in business, over which those who participate have no real (or at least very limited) control. Put simply, it is a political and economic environment that values, and above all applauds, *profits earned from commercial activities*. It is much less concerned with the consequences of those activities for consumers.

The first task in developing an integrated theory of the influences of globally distributed media content, therefore, is to explain what activities must be accomplished for that profit goal to be achieved. Fortunately, there is no need to invent an economic theory of capitalism in order to provide that explanation. That was accomplished in a classical sense more than two centuries ago.

MAKING A PROFIT IN A CAPITALISTIC ECONOMIC SYSTEM

The basics are these: Contemporary corporations compete to earn profits by producing and marketing goods and services. If they do not earn those profits for their owners and investors, they do not survive. That simple fact applies to those who produce media products for global markets as well as to producers of anything else sold in that marketplace. The question is, then, what are the requirements for making profits that are imposed by a political economy based on capitalism?

The basic features of capitalism as a political and economic system were first laid out in the last half of the eighteenth century by Adam Smith. This was at the dawn of the Industrial Revolution. Even today, Smith remains the towering figure providing an understanding of how that system works. Indeed, in spite of its many modifications by a host of governments, regulators and various others since Smith's time, the theories, concepts and principles he set forth remain as the essential explanation of the free market system within which profits can be made for investors through the production and distribution of goods.

Particularly well known is Adam Smith's foundation work, *An Inquiry into the Nature and Causes of the Wealth of Nations,* published in 1776.[2] It sets forth a basic understanding of political capitalism. The term "political capitalism" refers to an economic system that is regulated, and often supported by, a set of laws and regulations promulgated by governing authorities. It is that combination of government regulation and economic laws that remain today as the environment within which profits can be made (or not made) by those who own, control or direct global mass media organizations.

The "Invisible Hand" Controlling the Marketplace

Of particular interest for understanding the functioning of the contemporary global media industries—as well as for interpreting the findings revealed by the present project—is Smith's explanation of the "invisible hand"governing the marketplace. Smith used this colorful phrase to describe a set of natural economic "forces" and "laws" (orderly relationships) that in a capitalistic system determine the nature and consequences of the link between *competition* and *monopoly*.

The central ideas of the "invisible hand" are not difficult to understand. Essentially, they explain what political and economic conditions producers must cope with if they expect to earn profits. Whether they will be successful in reaching that goal or not depends upon two major factors. One is whether they have a *monopoly*—enabling them to produce and market a product that is highly desired by the consumers to which the product is sold, but which is produced by no one else. Obviously, that is the ideal situation for a producer. As Smith noted:

> The monopolists, by keeping the market understocked, by never fully supplying the effectual demand, sell their commodities much above the natural price, and raise their emoluments greatly above their natural rate. The price of monopoly is upon every occasion the highest which can be got.[3]

Smith recognized very clearly that while the existence of a monopoly benefitted the producer, it did not do so for the society, the consumers or the workers (who did not receive corresponding increases in wages) for producing the commodity.

A second factor in the invisible hand is the far more common situation where there are multiple producers of the product or commodity. It is in this situation of *competition,* Smith explained, that the "iron hand" has its greatest influence:

> The market price of every commodity is regulated by the proportion between the quantity which is actually brought to market, and the demand of those who are willing to pay the natural price of the commodity [to cover costs] which must be paid to bring it thither.[4]

The factors of monopoly versus competition, then, govern prices. These factors provide a set of "laws" that determine the success or failure an enterprise that produces a product in an effort to make a profit. These laws do not represent moral choices or ethical options. If they work in favor of a producer, the enterprise is profitable. If not, it fails.

There are reasons why Smith's analysis of the "invisible hand" does not apply fully to the business of producing popular culture and entertainment products for a world market. His eighteenth century analysis for the most part was based on such products as grain and other agricultural commodities, or simple items like pins or cloth that were manufactured in the early factories. His was a time when the Industrial Revolution had barely begun.

Thus, one of the factors missing in his analysis is *quality*—a third factor that can have a profound influence on success or failure. That is, not all forms of a commodity are equal. For example, even in a saturated market, consumers may be willing to pay more for a product that they view as having higher quality. Presumably, it is for that reason today that some products are more successful than others. For example, in a sea of available automobiles, wines or shirts, some consumers are more willing to purchase, or in some cases willing to pay premium prices for, those that they believe stand out in quality. An important part of the "invisible hand," then, that Smith did not consider would be the *quality* that consumers perceive in the products that are offered to them by their producers.

Competition, as Smith's second major factor, is linked closely to the issue of perceived quality. The producer who is able to supply a product that consumers think is somehow better will win in the competition. That has clearly been the case in the production of at least some modern products. For example, such producers as tobacco companies and fast food chains compete ruthlessly for customers. To sell more of their products they offer various claims or larger and larger portions of what they produce. But contrary to the conclusions reached by Adam Smith, in some cases that competitive practice *harms* consumers, rather than benefits them. Obviously, he could not anticipate our increasing problems of lung cancer or obesity.

The Problem of "Quality"

In terms of the present analysis of media content, what is "quality" and how do consumers detect it? In media entertainment products, "quality" is (literally) in the eye of the beholder! That is, a given movie, television series, or even news account may be more or less *desirable* (be of higher "quality") insofar as it is more pleasing, fulfilling or gratifying to those who attend to it than other options available to them at the time. Thus, producers of this type of product still cannot escape the influences of the "invisible hand," in which competition for the attention of consumers (and profits that such attention generates) continue to play a controlling part. However, quality—in the sense of being perceived as desirable by those who pay—can be a critical factor. Thus, if a producer can figure out a way to offer a *better quality* product—perceived as more desirable by consumers—compared to those of the competition, and, of course, offer it at a price consumers will accept, that will increase market share and consequently profits.

Thus, Adam Smith's "invisible hand" of supply and demand—modified in terms of the factor of perceived quality—still plays a central role in determining who will or will not survive. Even though they were envisioned long ago, these principles continue to rule the marketplace. Today in a global environment of economic competition, those who design, develop and distribute media products (with the necessary quality) operate within just such a system. As noted, it is one over which they, in fact, have only limited control.

Essentially, then, this means that they must pay constant attention to consumer tastes and interests because "quality" in this global media marketplace is defined as "what the consumers want." If they like opera or classic music, that is what will be produced and sold. It their tastes are predominantly for slapstick movies, simple romance themes or musical extravaganzas, those will be designed, developed and distributed. If, on the other hand, the global audience wants graphic violence, criminal plots, explicit depictions of sex and dirty language, that is the form that "quality" will take. Failure to provide what their market wants spells financial disaster.

The "Inner Man" as "Internal Spectator"

Defining "quality" in terms of the wants and desires of consumers—as opposed to using abstract or more universal standards—poses an interesting dilemma for those who set out to produce and market popular culture to a global audience. What happens, for example, if the consumers in that global market want media content that has *harmful consequences* of which the producers are aware? That is scarcely a new or novel situation. It is not difficult today to identify products that are produced that can have harmful effects on those who buy and use them and for which their producers are fully aware of those consequences.

Actually, Adam Smith considered exactly that same issue, even before he wrote his famous analysis of the *Wealth of Nations*. Far less known, but very relevant to the present discussion, is his earlier work, *The Theory of Moral Sentiments,* which was first published in 1759.[5] The central issue addressed in that work concerned "human nature"—a very popular topic, not only now, but among philosophers of Smith's time and among a lengthy list extending back to Plato and Aristotle.

The most central issue in the analysis of "human nature" has long been, and remains, the factor of personal freedom of "choice." Philosophers for centuries have maintained that human beings have the *personal power of choice,* often called "free will." That is, they have the acquired, or have an inborn ability (some say God-given), to decide, within themselves, whether or not to commit an act that deviates from the norms and moral requirements of their society. That factor of choice has been the foundation of *criminal law* for centuries. It is embedded in the legal principle that a criminal act occurs when a person "knows the right, but chooses wrong to do."

Exceptions to the principle have long been made for those found to be without full mental capacity (the "insane") and those too young to have acquired the needed understanding of what constitutes proscribed conduct ("juveniles"), or even those who have been swept up in overpowering emotions of the moment (by an "irresistible impulse"). The same idea of "free will" and the ability to select the moral path has also provided the foundation for *codes of ethics* of various professions. For example, the Hippocratic Oath of the physician states as its most essential proposition: "First, do no harm."

Smith understood well that the pursuit of profits could easily intrude upon ethical considerations where one person is pitted competitively against another as each seeks maximum benefits. It was that factor, he maintained, that led societies to develop *institutions* (such as law and courts) by which the tendency to cross proscribed lines could be mitigated. Even so, the drive for profits—and the personal rewards that accrue from them—remain as powerful motivations that can influence the decisions of those who produce for the marketplace. That fact is abundantly illustrated in contemporary business news in the United States every day.

The most significant force keeping self-interest in control, Smith maintained, was the presence within each person of an "inner man." That inner person plays the part of an "internal spectator" of our conduct for each of us, approving or condemning decisions and actions that we perform. We would probably call it "conscience" today. Essentially, then, each person is his or her own *moral authority*—assessing whether the actions or decision he or she takes will or will not create harm to others.

These abstractions concerning the "invisible hand" and the "inner man" pose a true dilemma for those who produce and distribute a long list of products that can harm people. Some products obviously do so—such as crack cocaine, marijuana and "Saturday-night-specials" (cheap hand guns). Others may be less obviously harmful—such as alcoholic beverages, cigarettes and even soft drinks and Big Macs. In each case, however, the "inner man," presumably dwelling within each of those that produce and distribute such products, must wrestle with the dilemma of *maximizing profits*, but possibly at the expense of *creating harm*.

But is it realistic to suggest that such a dilemma may be relevant to those who design, develop and distribute mass communicated entertainment products to young people in societies around the globe? If, indeed, those activities do have harmful consequences, the answer would appear to be "yes." For that reason, the analysis of Adam Smith in his *Theory of Moral Sentiments* becomes directly relevant to the decisions and actions of those that produce and distribute media entertainment products and even news on a global basis.

But exactly how do these abstractions apply to those who make the decisions for those multinational corporations that produce and supply mass communications and popular culture to teenagers in societies like Saudi Arabia. or South Korea? Can they say, "we had no idea" (harm was being done) and "we were only following orders" (to make a profit)?

The answer is that they cannot ethically use these excuses *if they are aware, and understand fully, that what they are producing and distributing is indeed creating harm*. Moreover, if those who use the products (the audiences) are *unaware* of their effects, the producers have an additional responsibility. In the present case, that would appear to be true if their products are shaping the beliefs and attitudes of youth in those countries in such a way as to create false, negative and harmful images of what American people are like. Under those circumstances, Smith's principles from Moral Sentiments apply directly and forcibly to them.

The problem with that conclusion is that those in charge of production and distribution of such materials also may have no real understanding of the harmful consequences of their activities. They can rightly say, "we are just giving people what they want" ("just following orders" to make profits). Tailoring the product to the interests and tastes of the consumers is, after all, the definition of *perceived quality* that we noted. In that sense it is central to success within the context of the invisible hand.

Indeed, that excuse has merit insofar as there has been little in the way of solid research that demonstrates fully that harmful consequences do occur as a result of worldwide distribution of mass communications depicting the American people in flawed ways. Many critics have made claims that global media are harmful. Some have complained that consolidation of ownership will reduce the robust nature of issues in the news and limit the voices of diversity.[6] Others have been vocal critics of profit-making by the mass media who have proceeded from an *a priori* foundation of claims, conjectures and conclusions derived from the writings of Karl Marx. Many in business pay little attention to such objections.

Whatever their premises or political positions, such critics have seldom based their objections on a body of empirical findings assembled through the use of scientific research strategies. For that reason, many in the media, and many media scholars, see the array of different charges made by such critics as based on *emotional* commitments rather than factual evidence. What is needed, then, is a *substantial accumulation of research findings* that will better indicate whether or not the content of mass communication products currently being distributed worldwide for profit are actually creating harmful consequences for the American population.

The results presented in earlier sections of this report certainly suggest that. However, no claim can be made that the findings developed in the present project provide an adequate or compelling accumulation of research results. At best, they represent only a modest start. In other words, the results of the present study of teenage beliefs and attitudes need to be confirmed by a body of additional empirical evidence on the influence of global media content on teenage attitudes. If that can be accomplished, then the producers of that content would have to reconcile the dilemma between their actions to increase market share in response to the "invisible hand" and the assessments of that conduct by their "internal observer."

THE MARKET:
DEMOGRAPHIC CHARACTERISTICS OF THE GLOBAL AUDIENCE

Adam Smith understood the problems of operating a business very well. First, one must understand the nature of the *market*. That is, who are the people who can be expected to purchase the product that will be produced? If the producer hasn't a clue as to their nature, or what they want, then the business has little chance of succeeding. An important question for the producers of globally distributed mass communicated products today, then, is *who makes up that audience* and *what do they want?*

The answer to those questions begins with an understanding of the composition of the world's populations, and especially those categories of people in various countries who are most likely to attend to and enjoy media entertainment content and popular culture. In that sense, the "who" question has a simple answer. *It is the young.*

Every conceivable audience survey, poll, focus group, or other research procedure in virtually every country for decades has verified that those who go to the cinema most often, who view he most popular televison programs, and who are most devoted to popular music and celebrity performers are those who are 19 years old or younger—essentially teenagers. As people get older, get married, enter the labor force and have families, they pay less and less attention to the latest songs, performers, stars, movie idols, sex symbols, rap artists, fashion trends and "in"celebrities. Popular culture, in short, is a world that is familiar to and enthusiastically consumed by the young. It is of less interest to older people. The answer to "who," then, is that the audience for media-delivered popular culture and entertainment are in large part *those who are in their teens.*

Given that rather obvious situation, a second question is this: Among the world's population, how many of the people on the planet are, in fact, teenagers? Moreover, how is that age category distributed globally? For example, in which countries, where the producers of media entertainment content distribute their products, are there concentrations of teenagers? This is an important question for defining the market for popular culture. Thus, the age composition of populations in various countries is essential information for those who must decide what to produce and where to distribute it.

Numerical data about the inhabitants of countries is developed by *demographers*—those who systematically study how many people of different characteristics (age, sex, education, income, etc.) are present in populations. As noted, of particular interest for present purposes is the composition of populations in terms of age. Fortunately, most of the countries in the world keep accurate demographic statistics by conducting a periodic *census.*

The idea of a census of a population started long ago. In ancient times, counts were made of families to determine who could serve in the army, who could labor in public projects, or who could pay more taxes. Long before the birth of Christ, surveys were taken for such purposes in ancient Babylonia, Palestine, Persia and China. In the year 5 B.C., for example, such counts were made across the entire Roman Empire. In more recent times, beginning in the eighteenth century, countries routinely counted their inhabitants and enumerated different categories of people in various versions of modern census-taking. Today, that practice is virtually universal in all but the least developed nations.

This type of census-derived information makes it possible to determine the age composition of populations in different types of countries around the world. In particular, demographers note significant differences in the age composition of *developed* countries (basically those that are industrialized) and those that are

Figure 28: POPULATION PYRAMIDS

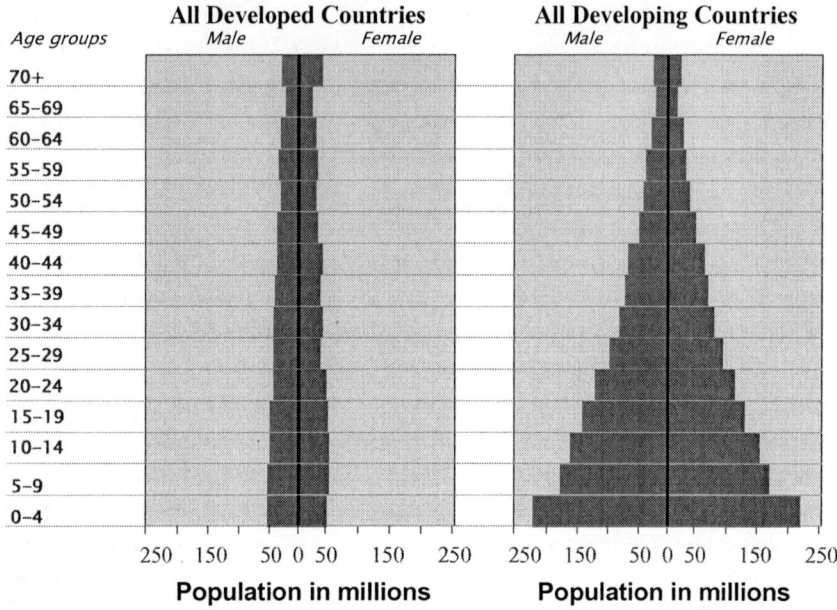

developing. By comparing these two categories of countries in terms of the age composition of their populations, an important question can be answered concerning the global market for media-delivered popular culture. Stated simply, where are those markets? The answer is that those countries with the largest concentrations of teenagers make up the largest market for such products.

Figure 28 shows the difference in the age composition of the contemporary *developed* vs the *developing* countries. These two charts are what demographers call *population pyramids*. Note that they show the millions of persons present in the combined populations of the two categories of countries by both age and gender. For example, in the combined developed countries there are slightly more than 50 million males and about the same number of females in the youngest age category (that includes those who were just born up to those who are 4 years old). Taken together these very young children add up to about 100 million new inhabitants. That can be compared to the approximately 225 million males and a similar number of females in that same category for the developing countries. Taken together, these countries have nearly half a billion (450 million) very young children.[7]

Moving up the steps in the pyramids to the age categories most relevant to the producers of media-delivered popular culture (the two categories between 10 and 19), the developed countries have a total of about 200 million teenagers. That is a lot, but by contrast, the developing countries have a total of more than 600 million—three times as many. It does not, as they say, "take a rocket scientist" to figure out where the greatest numbers of potential customers for entertainment media designed for youthful consumers are located. In part, then, these demographic data provide an answer to the question of "who" will pay for media entertainment products.

But what about the future? There are, in fact, remarkable changes taking place in many of the world's populations. In the Western countries—especially those in Europe—significant trends in demographic composition are taking place.[8] Simply put, their populations are getting older and older. Fertility rates (the number of children born to women of child-bearing age) across Europe are now so low that the continent's population is likely to drop markedly in the years ahead. This means that fewer and fewer children are being added to the population.

Moreover, people are living longer and longer. These trends will pose severe economic problems for countries like Germany, Italy and other members of the European Union. The percent of older citizens in such countries will rise to the point that fewer and fewer younger workers will be supporting more and more of the aged, who draw government-backed pensions. A third factor is that many of these Western countries have strong controls over immigration, which could bring in more of the young.

For the present project these trends mean that there will be smaller and smaller markets for popular culture and sexy, violent, crime-focused media entertainment content in Western countries. Those who produce such entertainment materials will be increasingly dependent on non-Western markets, whose populations will continue to be dominated by the young. Taking all of these trends together, then, it seems likely that producers will have to increase their dependence on youths in non-Western countries if they expect to increase their profits. To do this they will use production strategies that emphasize the themes that attract and gratify youthful audiences.

Among those audiences, one problem that producers of popular culture may face is *disposable income*. That is, while there may be nearly a billion teenagers in both the developed and developing countries, and many more to come, can they all pay for the products that they consume? Do they have the money to go to the cinema, to purchase the CDs, rent the VCR tapes to view movies at home, etc.? The answer here is a guarded "yes." We are not talking about the purchase of Rolex watches, BMWs or other luxury products with high price tags. Most teenagers in the developed countries have at least some modest income provided by parents (or from other sources) for such purposes.

In the developing countries, where teenage funds are more limited, going to the movies costs much less than in the United States, and a VCR tape can be rented on the streets for a fraction of what it would cost in an American city. Thus, even though any particular teenager in a developed or developing country may have only limited disposable income, added together across the globe the nearly one billion who enjoy popular culture represents a huge pool of money from which profits can be derived.

It makes sense, then, for those multinational corporations who produce mass communication entertainment content to focus their attention on the truly massive numbers of young people whose tastes and interests will generate the largest audiences and profits for them. The older generations, in both the developed and developing countries, are preoccupied with work, family and other adult responsibilities. These lead them away from preoccupation with the latest entertainment celebrity, TV drama or the fad in popular music. Those who produce popular culture and entertainment products understand these issues. Their definitions of "quality," in terms of what they produce, is whatever will capture and hold the attention of this huge pool of young people. If they failed to understand this, as Adam Smith pointed out long ago, they would be overwhelmed by their competitors.

MEDIA DEPENDENCE ON POPULAR CULTURE

As noted earlier, the results of this project, presented in previous chapters, can be interpreted and explained within an *integrated theory* that brings together a multi-stage sequence of explanations of background events, audience behavior and consequent media influences.

The above discussion of the requirements for profit-making in a capitalistic political economy (as analyzed by Adam Smith), plus the consideration of how to define quality in terms of the demographic characteristics of the global audience, represents only the initial part of that sequence. The next stage to be discussed draws upon a rather specific mass communication theory that explains how contemporary mass media are *dependent upon the production and distribution of popular culture.*

The term "popular culture," sometimes referred to as *mass* culture, has many meanings. In its broadest sense, it refers to forms of art, entertainment and diversion developed for unsophisticated people in a society, as opposed to "elite culture" produced for those who prefer more complex forms. The origins of the term "mass" (or popular) culture are said to be in the two German terms *Masse* and *Kulture*:

> The mass is (or was) the nonaristocratic, uneducated portion of European society, especially the people who today might be described as lower-middle class, working class and poor. *Kultur* translates as *high culture*; it refers not only to the art, music, literature and other symbolic products that were (and are) preferred by the well-educated elite of European society but also to the styles of thought and the feelings of those who choose these products—those who are "cultured." Mass culture, on the other hand, refers to the symbolic products used by the "uncultured" majority.[9]

While human beings have always enjoyed light entertainment, unsophisticated art, simple diversions and sports, popular culture played only a minor role in the economic affairs of societies until relatively recent times. Before the Industrial Revolution, most ordinary people toiled from daylight to dark on their farms, or at other forms of work. They had little leisure time to enjoy entertainment, so there was no great need for popular culture.

With the coming of the Industrial Revolution, factory work became scheduled rigidly by the clock and people began to have at least some leisure time and at least some disposable income to purchase diversion. However, sources of amusement were fewer than they are now. There was no cinema, phonograph, radio or television. People could turn to print media if they were literate. Or, if they had an afternoon or day off they could attend ball games, circuses, amusement parks, dance halls, roller skating rinks, and so on.

As factories prospered, people concentrated in cities. Then, as leisure time slowly began to increase, there was a growing need for simple and cheap forms of diversion that working families that could enjoy at home, or by traveling a short distance and paying a modest fee. The movies that came in the early 1900s provided just such entertainment. Thus, the availability of popular culture began to increase after the turn of the century.

Soon came home radio, with its soap operas, quiz shows, evening drama, comics, sports broadcasts, and other forms of entertainment. With each additional medium came an increasing flood of popular culture fare. After television arrived, the airways were flooded with sports, sitcoms, daytime serials, old movies and cartoons. The Age of Popular Culture had become a reality. After cable, the VCR and the Internet joined the available media, the pace increased even further.

In modern times, then, and especially after the development of mass media, popular culture became a *manufactured product developed to make a profit by being marketed to the less sophisticated parts of the population.* It became, in other words, the amusements and diversions enjoyed by the rank-and-file of ordinary people.

These same trends are taking place in less developed societies. The family living in a small agricultural village in the Middle East, in Africa, Asia or Latin America is just as fascinated with popular culture as one dwelling in a working-class neighborhood in Chicago. During the twentieth century, the media by which such families could receive and enjoy the manufactured products of popular culture spread into all parts of the globe.

Thus, as a result of the worldwide adoption of communication technologies, even people in a small, remote and dusty village in Pakistan have access to a television set, probably equipped with a satellite dish and a VCR receiver. In some cases it may even be hooked to a cable. The system will be owned either collectively by the residents of the village, or by one of the more prosperous residents who allows access by neighbors—but in either case it will be located where it can be viewed by a number of people. That site will serve both as a social center and as a nightly source of entertainment for both young and old.[10]

Villagers in such circumstances are likely to receive television programs originating in the United States. Few will receive media entertainment content that originates in their own country due to limited local facilities for production. Those who live in more urban settings are likely to have their own, (or shared) TV receivers that are similarly equipped at home.

What both rural and urban residents receive may be broadcasts over the air from a local station, possibly transmitted over a national cable system or sent by a TV network via satellite from outside the country. Movies on VCR tape will readily available. These will originate mainly from western sources, especially from producers in the United States. Some will have local language subtitles. Others will not, but will be interesting in any case, especially if they have a lot of action and depictions of people engaging in activities unlikely to be seen locally.

Popular culture, then, is a product of a population's dependency on mass communication as a source of diversion and gratification. In many ways it is replacing the ability to gratify needs for diversion by informal social contacts with family and neighbors. Societies in all parts of the world today require a relentless flow of unsophisticated entertainment content. The production of that content defines the characteristics of the competitive struggle among media producers for audience attention.

Another issue related to popular culture concerns its relationship to, and influence upon, high culture. Many critics refer to popular culture as *kitsch*—entertainment products that have no redeeming artistic or educational value. Kitsch is often described as cheap and tawdry by the standards of the elite, but it is satisfying and fully enjoyed by the masses.

Critics also point out that popular culture often "mines" its themes, motifs, plots, musical scores and other features of its content from elite or high culture. Thus, the plot of a motion picture, the drama of a soap opera, or the story told in a cheap novel, may be a watered down version of something that can be found in Shakespeare. The latest popular tune may incorporate musical sequences from a sonata originally created by Beethoven, and so on. Moreover, say critics, the "heroes" of popular culture are created merely by media exposure and not by doing significant deeds. Real-life heroes are persons who made a significant contribution to their society by brave or daring action, not by singing, dancing, acting or strumming on a guitar. Thus, by promoting media-created "heroes of consumption," popular culture is said to diminish the stature of "heroes of the deed."

Taking these features and criticisms into account, the relationship between the audience, the media and popular culture can be summarized in a very simple way. A theory of media dependency on popular culture helps to explain both the sources of such content and its influences on the public.[11] Its basic propositions are these:

1. Our privately owned media, functioning within a capitalistic economic system, are dedicated to maximizing their profits by presenting *popular culture* that will increase audience attention, interest, circulations, viewers and listeners.

2. This locks them into an *economic dependency* on attracting and holding the attention of the largest number of people who make up the potential media audience.

3. The members of the audience rely on the media to offer a broad range of entertainment content, consistent with their interests and tastes, to *fill their leisure time* in gratifying ways—but content that makes limited intellectual demands on its consumers.

4. The content that has greatest appeal to the largest number of people in the audience is what some term *kitsch*—popular culture entertainment products with limited redeeming artistic value, but which command wide attention of, and gratification for, the audience.

5. **Therefore**, the economic forces and consumer taste systems driving the media result in a constant production and dissemination of kitsch. The consequences may be driving out high culture, elevating the status of media-created celebrities and diminishing or obscuring the recognition of real-life heroes.

The theory of audience and media dependency on popular culture helps in understanding why it is that those who produce and distribute mass communications must develop and disseminate content that will be acceptable, interesting and gratifying to their audiences. As discussed earlier, in most populations in the world, these are young people, in age categories 19 or below. They are neither well-educated, economically affluent nor interested in content at higher levels of taste.

Even if the theory is assumed to be essentially correct, however, it does not answer another question. That is, *what must those who distribute popular culture produce to earn and maintain a competitive edge*? That is, no single multinational corporation producing entertainment products has a monopoly (with the advantages outlined by Adam Smith). Indeed, the small number that prepare popular culture for the global market are in intense competition (with all of the attendant problems outlined by Smith). As a consequence, as explained earlier, careful attention must be paid by those producers to *perceived quality*.

In this context that means developing content that will (1) capture and hold the attention of, (2) be seen as pleasing by and (3) provide gratification for, the youthful population that constitutes the global audience. The greater the extent to which these "quality" features of content can be developed, the more likely it will be that a given producer/distributor will achieve economic success.

But how can this goal be achieved? It has already been explained that the content produced cannot be at a highbrow level, but must have other kinds of features—qualities that will be especially appealing to the young in the societies where the products will be marketed. It requires no great insight to understand that the various corporations producing and marketing entertainment products constantly seek competitive ways to interest and satisfy their young audiences. What that means, simply put, is producing content with themes, plots and depictions that young people will enjoy, even though it may annoy older people. This means content focusing on action, portrayals of crime, situations of danger, graphic violence, open sex and coarse language.

THE CREEPING CYCLE OF DESENSITIZATION

As competition for youthful markets increases, then, "improvements" must be made in the "quality" of what is offered as media entertainment and popular culture to the youthful audience. New kinds of content must be produced that will succeed in holding and hopefully enlarging audiences for the products produced. For these basic reasons, producers are in a situation where, to continue to make profits in a competitive environment, they must constantly *exceed the normative limits of conservative acceptability* concerning controversial themes.

However, that is not always possible, especially in societies where portrayals of crime, violence, sex and vulgarity are not tolerated well. To get around those limits, producers use a simple strategy. They include as much of this content that will appeal to their youthful audience as they can. If they transgress the norms of a society and come under strong criticism, they will hold the line until things settle down—until the relevant public comes to accept the transgressions. They may even retreat a bit. When the level of criticism dies down—and the public is "desensitized" to what is being offered—they push over the line once again.

Thus, there appears to be a kind of "creeping cycle" brought about by the competitive nature of the business. The limits of acceptability in content are approached, and then crossed. If nothing happens, the lines are pushed farther—with more violence, crime, sex and vulgarities. In this way, the cycle repeats: If critics become particularly vocal and outcries from conservative people appear to threaten profitability, then a temporary retreat is made—only to be reversed when the clamor dies down. It is, of course the youthful nature of the audience that drives this process. The "creeping cycle of desensitization" theory can be stated in terms of the following five propositions:

1. The communication industries produce entertainment products within a system of economic capitalism, in which making profits is an essential and highly approved goal.

2. The types of products that attract the attention of the largest numbers in the audience (largely the young) are those that emphasize socially controversial themes that transgress conservative norms, such as sensationalism, crime, sex, violence and vulgarity.

3. Producers in the United States enjoy the protections of the First Amendment to the Constitution, so there are few legal or political restraints on what content can be designed, developed and distributed.

4. For that reason, producers of media content—seeking ever-larger audiences and profits in a highly competitive economic, but protected, environment—will constantly increase depictions of sensational topics, crime, sex, violence and vulgarity, until public protests arise.

5. **Therefore**, when public outcry threatens their industry, the producers will stop, or even temporarily reverse, their transgressions of norms until things calm down; but in a creeping cycle of desensitization, the producers will move the cutting edge of transgressions forward again as soon as the protests becomes muted.

The creeping cycle theory provides insights into the ways in which producers manage to survive and prosper in a highly competitive market by increasing the desirability of their products to their consumers. As noted, improving the "quality" of one's product over that of competitors is a standard strategy in a capitalistic system. However, both the theory of media dependence on popular culture and the creeping cycle explanation provide little in the way of understanding the mass communication process from the point of view of the consumer. That is, why is it that youthful audiences are drawn to the kinds of media entertainment and popular culture that earns high profits from those that produce it? In other words, what motivates them to attend?

SEEKING GRATIFICATION FROM MEDIA ENTERTAINMENT

The answer to that motivation question requires that an additional theory be added to the integrated sequence being developed. It is a theory that has long been standard in the field of mass communication studies. It seeks to explain the reasons for which individuals in audiences (in general) seek out and attend to various forms of media content. In a selective manner, some seem to find enjoyment in viewing spectator sports on television. Others enjoy romance movies, or professional wrestling. Still others seek out and obtain satisfactions from listening to favorite performers of popular music.

In that sense, it is a general motivational theory applying to virtually all forms of media content and all audiences, rather than one that applies specifically to the global distribution of popular culture. Originally, it was developed as an alternative to the idea that people in audiences (in the United States) passively attended to whatever the media happened to be offering, in a non-selective way.

That older idea has been termed the "Magic Bullet Theory" and it has long since been abandoned.

Originally, the *Uses for Gratification Theory,* described below, explained media attention as a consequence of audience members seeking to satisfy various kinds of *psychological needs*—a standard way of explaining motivation. However, that link, between specific human needs and specific media content that will provide gratification for those needs, has been difficult to demonstrate. For that reason, the theory remains somewhat controversial.

Nevertheless, the basic idea has merit. In other words, audiences actively select and attend to a specific form of media content because by so doing they gain some form of *gratification* from that experience. That is, they enjoy it, like it or otherwise find it satisfying. For youthful audiences in counties around the world, those gratifications may take many forms. Attending to popular culture may simply be a means of having fun, of sharing a world with youthful peers in which adults are excluded, or of having experiences that provide a thrill of forbidden activities in a conservative society, In any case, the uses for gratification theory can be summarized in the following way:

1. Audience members do not wait passively to attend to whatever forms of content and programming that the media happen to transmit.

2. Consumers of mass communications have a structure of motivating needs that they seek to gratify through various kinds of experiences.

3. Those needs have been shaped by the individual's inherited nature as well as by his or her learning experiences within a web of social relationships and social category memberships.

4. Their structure of needs leads audience members actively to seek specific forms of media content that can provide diversion, entertainment, or other kinds of satisfactions.

5. **Therefore,** members of the audience actively select and then attend to specific forms of media content that provide gratifications that fulfill their needs.

In the present context, those forms of media content that provide gratification are the kinds of movies, TV programs, musical recordings, radio programming or other types of popular culture to which young people across the globe are drawn. It is not a complex idea, and it appears intuitively to be consistent with the realities of youthful attention to the entertainment products that are produced and distributed by the multinational corporations who supply them. Moreover, it does provide a simple explanation of the initial stage that focuses on the audience in the overall theory of the media influence process being discussed.

THE PROCESS OF INCIDENTAL LEARNING

A second issue with respect to the audience, once they have selected what they want from the media content available to them, is what they acquire or learn from the experience of viewing, listening or reading. Some of what they acquire may be trivial, and have very little influence. But other media experiences may have a significant effect on individuals. They may see a situation that brings them to adopt a new form of behavior, a new way of dressing, a new hair style, or a different way of thinking about other kinds of people. In particular, learning by observing the actions of other people (directly, or from media) can bring about such influences.

Psychologist Albert Bandura calls this process *social learning*. His social learning theory has important applications to the study of media effects through what is called "modeling theory," which was developed in the 1960s.[12]

For present purposes, an important form of social learning is one that takes place almost *accidentally* when people observe the behavior, characteristics and social relationships of people depicted in various settings in mass communications. Recognizing the consequences of what is called *incidental learning* has long been central to efforts to assess the effects of the visual media—particularly television and motion pictures—that present visual portrayals of people acting out social roles and other forms of behavior.

Wilbur Schramm and his colleagues developed the concept of incidental learning in 1961, when they turned their attention to the influences of television programs on American children at a time when the medium had only recently arrived. The influences of this new medium were under intense scrutiny at the time.

Most of a child's learning from television, as we have said, is *incidental learning*. By this we mean learning that takes place when a viewer goes to television for entertainment and stores up certain items of information without seeking them. Practically all of a child's early use of television is in a quest for entertainment. Indeed, he is introduced to the mass media as vehicles of entertainment: to tell him a story or make him laugh, or to bring him one of his favorite performers.[13]

Needless to say, this type of learning is not confined to viewing television. It can take place from any medium. The main point is that such learning is *subtle* and *unwitting*. It takes place when a person goes to media content for gratification and diversion. That individual has no intention of being "instructed" by whatever he or she is viewing, reading or hearing, and indeed may have no realization that such instruction is taking place. Nevertheless, while being entertained, the person acquires understandings, knowledge and beliefs about whatever situations, people and their characteristics that are embedded in the media portrayals.

A second important feature of incidental learning is that the lessons supplied by the media content *have not been deliberately placed there* by those professional communicators who design, develop and disseminate that content. They may have no intention of producing "instructional materials," and may have no realization that they are doing so. Moreover, in their exercise of "artistic freedom" as they create characters, plots and depictions of actions, they may have no concern that what they show in their product is a factual reflection of reality. Their goal is solely to create entertainment products that will attract and please their audiences (for the purposes of making a profit). Indeed, as noted, they are required to do exactly that if they expect to retain their jobs. If American characters are shown in their films, TV programs and so forth, in ways that depict them very negatively, that's "show business."

Regardless of the intentions of either party, however, the consequences of these incidental lessons can be truly important. As audiences seek gratification, they unwittingly acquire beliefs and understandings about whatever is depicted in the content. Needless to say, that knowledge may be seriously inaccurate.

The process of incidental learning, then, provides a key to understanding why teenagers in other countries—who seek gratification from movies, television programming and other forms of popular culture—encounter *flawed images* of Americans. Those images have been prepared in Western societies by people exercising their creative talents to produce content that will be enjoyed by their youthful audiences. Only if they have that "quality" will those products earn the needed profits. Depicting actual reality—showing the nature of most ordinary Americans—by producing completely accurate (but dull) instructional materials is their least concern

For that reason, their entertainment products focus on whatever will produce gratification—themes, plots, actions, characters and other content that will be exciting and fun. The incidental result, however, is that what they design, develop and distribute can provide seriously inaccurate lessons that portray ordinary Americans in unrealistic and often very negative ways.

A good example of the incidental learning process is provided by a recent study of the influence of depictions of smoking in movies reported in *Lancet*, a major British medical journal.[14] Exposure to smoking depicted in movies was assessed among a total of 3,547 youths (10-14). These were youngsters who reported in a preliminary survey that they had never tried smoking.

Then, the exposure of these subjects to films showing people smoking was assessed. A total of 50 recent movies were randomly selected and the number of times actors were shown smoking in these films was determined. Most of the original youths (73 percent) were contacted a second time, 13 to 26 months later, to determine two things: One was to determine how many of these movies they had seen. The other was to determine how many had since started smoking.

The results indicated that there was an unmistakable relationship between exposure to the movie-portrayed smoking and taking up the habit. The relationship was strongest for those subjects whose parents did not smoke! Those who produced the movies may not have deliberately planned this; the kids who took up smoking were not aware of the influence of the incidental lessons embedded in the films.

The basic ideas of incidental learning theory can be summarized in the following set of propositions:

1. Those mass communicators who design, develop and distribute media entertainment content do so within a capitalistic system.

2. Within that system, few formal restrictions are imposed on the content that is produced and making profits is the first goal—that is, earning a maximum return on investment.

3. The media products produced and distributed are designed creatively to provide maximum gratification and entertainment for their audiences and there is little concern whether they provide accurate instructional lessons about the people depicted in their content.

4. The audiences who attend to those entertainment products do so for the purpose of being entertained and experiencing gratification—they often have no intention of receiving instruction or a realization that they are doing so.

5. **Therefore,** while attending, those audiences are unwittingly exposed to subtle but unintended lessons about the people, actions and situations that are depicted—from which they may acquire very flawed ideas, beliefs and understandings about those who are being portrayed.

Because of the importance of incidental lessons, this theory can be added as one more stage in the integrated explanation of media effects being developed. However, while the idea of unwitting and unintended lessons in media content provides a needed part of the overall process by which globally distributed mass communication content defines people who live in the United States, there is one additional stage that needs to be explained. That is, what happens when teenagers in another country actually encounter the incidental lessons placed before them? Do they understand that very few Americans are really as violent, sexually immoral and criminally inclined as those portrayed in movies, television programming and other forms of popular culture? Or, do they develop distorted views by incorporating into their beliefs and attitudes an image of the ordinary American as it is depicted in media entertainment content?

Another stage of the integrated theory of media influences being developed is one that explains that outcome. This stage can be described by using an explanation of human understanding and belief that originated in philosophy, centuries before anyone ever dreamed of something called mass communication. This process was later called *the social construction of reality*. Within the present context, it provides an explanation of what happens as a result of a teenagers receiving lessons about Americans (about whom they have no other sources of information) by absorbing the incidental instruction provided by media entertainment and popular culture.

THE SOCIAL CONSTRUCTION OF REALITY

More than two thousand years ago, Plato (427-347 BC), as well as other philosophers of the time, was perplexed by what are, even today, three very difficult questions.

The most basic was this: How is it that the many objects, events and situations that exist or take place in the world have come into *being*? What brought them to exist in reality and causes them to undergo various kinds of changes? Answers to this important question would come over the centuries from the physical and biological sciences.

Second, how is it that human beings can gain understandings and knowledge in their minds about those things and situations that are external to them? This is the question of *knowing*—that is, of developing internal representations of external reality (in our heads). Answers to this question, centuries later, would be provided by social and behavioral sciences, such as psychology.

Finally, Plato and a host of others sought answers to the ways in which internal knowledge about the world was translated into behavior. This is what they called the question of *doing*. In Plato's time, and even today, this poses the question of *ethical actions*—both on the part of individuals and the problem of developing and conducting systems of government that benefit the population and hold in check the unethical actions of a few.

Of importance to the present project is the second question—of how human beings develop *internal knowledge* of different features of the external world that is valid and accurate. One possible answer is that they do so through *direct sensory experience* with (seeing, hearing, touching) the events, objects and situations they encounter (which is widely accepted today). For Plato, however, this did not seem like a valid answer. He mistrusted that source of knowledge. A far better route, he believed, was to develop true and valid knowledge through the process of *using pure reason*.

To illustrate what he saw as the fallibility of depending on sensory experience as a basis for "knowing," he set forth in his *Republic* a description of an imaginary experiment. He intended his "Allegory of the Cave" as a illustration of how false interpretations of reality could be the result, if one relied only on what one could see and hear with the senses. But even though Plato's ideas eventually proved to be totally incorrect as explaining a route to valid knowledge, his famous description of what would take place—if his imaginary experiment in the cave were actually carried out—provides an important insight into how young people in societies round the world develop flawed images of ordinary Americans from media entertainment.

In *The Republic* Plato asks us to "Imagine the condition of [a small number] of men who had always lived deep within a sort of cavernous chamber underground, with an entrance open only to light and a long passage all down the cave."[15] We are also asked to imagine that these men had been chained to a bench since they were children. The bench backs up to a wall, located in such a way that the men can see only straight ahead.

Behind the men, a high wall runs down the middle of the cave. On the other side of the wall (opposite the chained men) is a kind of walkway raised up to within several feet from the top. This serves as a narrow track along which other men can walk while carrying various objects. The chained men on the other side cannot see those walking along the track because they are facing the other way, on the other side, and seeing only the wall of the cave in front of them. Now Plato wants us to imagine a very bright fire against the opposite side of the cave, whose light will be reflected onto the wall that the chained men can see.

With these conditions in place, imagine people walking along the track that the chained men cannot see. These men are holding up figures and shapes of various kinds. Some are silhouettes of animals and human beings. There are many other shapes. These are held up on poles just above the top of the wall. With the fire burning very brightly, its light can be seen glowing strongly against the wall of the cave that is visible to the chained men. What they see will be *shadows* (of the objects being held up). Those shadows will be cast on the wall in such a way that the seated men can clearly observe them. They will not see those holding up the silhouettes because they are below the top of the wall on the other side.

What did Plato imply here? He explained that the seated men must use their sensory experience to observe the shadows. The question, then, is how do they *interpret* what their sensory experience provides for them? Plato argued that the chained men would use their sensory experience to try construct *meanings* for what they were seeing—the only realities that they were able to experience with their senses. Indeed, he maintained, the chained men would *believe that the shadows were reality.*

They would invent shared rules for understanding and for evaluating them, and invent names for the different ones. In this way, the "knowing" that they developed, would be based solidly on their sensory experience. Needless to point out, Plato maintained, this would lead to a *very false view of reality.* Obviously, however, as the men discussed the shadows, and worked out shared rules of interpretation through communication they would developed *a (flawed) social construction of reality,* jointly formed, on which they agreed and which they shared.

To drive home his point (about the problem of depending solely on sensory experience), Plato now introduced a dramatic condition. We are asked to imagine that one of the chained men was suddenly set free. At first, he would be allowed to see everything in the cave—the wall, the walkway, the fire, the people carrying the silhouettes, and so on—the whole system by which the shadows had been produced. He would be shown that what he and his companions had been seeing was *only an illusion,* and what he was now experiencing was their actual nature. Later, he might be taken out of the cave and shown the world of everyday life in Greece at the time—a totally different reality. Gradually, said Plato, he would come to understand that what he was now seeing was indeed the true nature of reality, and that his earlier sensory experience had provided a completely flawed view of the world.

To conclude the experiment, Plato introduced still another dramatic condition. What would happen, he asked, if the newly freed man were taken back into the cave, to be chained again in his former place? What would be the consequence when the man tried to explain to his former companions that the reality they had socially constructed was not reality at all, and that it was only a false illusion? How would they react?

Plato believed that they would reject his explanations as those of a raving madman, and that they would laugh at him. They would regard him much as we view a person today who claims he was abducted by space aliens and taken to another planet where he was shown a very different reality. Plato also said that if the man made such claims, his companions would be likely to kill him.

The implications that can be drawn from Plato's allegory provide an important foundation on which at least some explanations of the process and influences of mass communication can be built. Plato was correct in concluding that people acquire conceptions of their physical and social world from others through a process of both observation and social communication. However, today, the social construction of reality is a process that takes place not only through interpersonal communication, but also when the media offer the only information available to them from which people can develop conceptions, beliefs, expectations and attitudes about various aspects of their physical and social world.

But how does this ancient but colorful allegory have relevance for the purposes of the present discussion? It takes no great stretch of the imagination to understand the experiences of a young person in Saudi Arabia or elsewhere, who may have no contact with actual Americans, but does have an abundance of incidental lessons embedded in media entertainment content from which to learn. Like the men in the cave, that teenager can see the "shadows" on the TV screen and at the cinema, and use them to develop a social construction of reality concerning the nature of Americans, their families, their typical behavior and their values. This explanation adds an important step to the multistage theory of media influences that is being developed. The propositions of the social construction theory can be stated as follows:

1. All human beings require *understandings* of the world in which they live, and to which they must adapt.

2. Communication through language became a part of human existence when evolutionary changes to the body made possible the control of sound with

the vocal chords and the storing of complex meanings in a larger brain.

3. With words and language available, features of the environment with which people had to deal could be given names, with associated conventions of internally aroused meanings, permitting *standardization of interpretations* of phenomena, stabilizing the meanings attached to all the aspects of reality with which people had to deal.

4. In modern times, *media*, including mass media, play a part in developing the meanings individuals acquire for events, situations and objects in the human environment through their depictions and representations in entertainment and other content.

5. **Therefore**, the meanings, either personal and private, or culturally shared, of any aspect of reality to which people must adjust, are developed in a process of interpersonal or mediated communication—indicating that reality, in the sense of individual interpretations (or a consensus of shared meanings) people attach to objects, actions, events and situations are *socially constructed.*

What this complex explanation means for the present task of bringing together a multistage theory of media influences is that audiences—whatever their nature—develop what Walter Lippman called "pictures in their heads of the world outside."[16] He used this colorful phrase in his discussion of the part played by news media in the society of his time (the 1920s), but obviously it is drawn directly from Plato's allegory explaining the social construction of reality.

In the present context, those "pictures in their heads" are evaluative beliefs, understandings, interpretations and consequent *attitudes* toward ordinary Americans. The social construction explanation adds an important step to the multistage theory of media influences that begins with corporations operating in the competitive environment analyzed by Adam Smith and ends with knowledge about Americans obtained from media depictions that provide vivid incidental lessons about their nature.

THE GRADUAL ACCUMULATION OF MINIMAL EFFECTS

There is, however, one last issue that should be considered. That is, in developing social constructions of reality about Americans, does it take place quickly—as a result of seeing a few movies or viewing a few TV dramas? Or, is that process that takes place slowly on the basis of a multitude of exposures?

There is ample reason to believe that learning to dislike or even hate Americans is a process in which exposure to popular culture is only one element. It must be stressed that the youth in countries around the world have many other sources of information that come to bear on them. These include families and in some societies the teachings of religious leaders. There are also peers, information supplied by governments and, of course, the news.

If definitions of Americans are consistent across these various sources, negative images may develop early and quickly. If not, the process may be slower. In any case, no single movie, television program, music video, computer game, news bulletin, government propaganda message or lesson from the temple, mosque or pulpit will transform the beliefs and attitudes of an individual from one view to another.

After several decades of intensive research, it is now widely accepted that any particular mass communicated message (e.g., movie or TV program) has only *selective* and *limited* effects on the media audience. Hundreds of experiments and other kinds of research studying persuasive messages aimed at changing people's beliefs, attitudes and behavior have revealed only minor influences on all of those who were exposed to such single messages.

At the same time, year-after-year, changes could be observed taking place in society that many scholars believed were significantly influenced by the media. Thus, there was a *dilemma* concerning the ability of the media to influence people's ideas and behavior. For example, it appeared to many observers that mass communication played a significant part in bringing about such changes as Richard Nixon's resignation due to the events of Watergate, the civil rights movement of the 1960s, the redefinition that took place in the United States of the Vietnam War, and many recent changes that have occurred related to health behavior, such as the use of seat belts in automobiles.

Clearly, some way of resolving this apparent dilemma was needed. Both the scientific research and the careful observation of historical events seemed to lead to sound conclusions—even if they were completely opposite. Finally, it was clear that almost all of the scientific research was based on *short-term* studies, making use of brief experiments and one-time surveys. The historical observations of changes in society *extended over time*. The resolution of the dilemma came when it was realized that both conclusions could be correct. In a short-term sense, the media may have very selective and limited influences. But over a long period, small changes occurring a few at a time can *eventually add up* to significant long-term influences.

Indeed, it was those issues on which the media focused *repeatedly* and in relatively *consistent* ways that changed people most over time. If those conditions prevailed, and if the various media—print, film and broadcast—*corroborated* each other by presenting the same interpretations, truly significant changes could take place in people's beliefs, attitudes and behavior. From these considerations the theory of *the accumulation of minimal effects* was developed. It is relevant to the present situation in which over time consistent incidental lessons are presented in the media that eventually bring about negative constructions of reality on the part of youthful audiences. The theory's basic assumptions and logical prediction are as follows:

1. The mass media begin to focus their attention on and transmit messages about a *specific topic* (some problem, situation or issue).

2. Over an extended period they continue to do so in a relatively *consistent* and *persistent* way and their presentations *corroborate* each other.

3. Individual members of an audience increasingly become *aware* of these messages and, on a person-by-person basis, a growing *comprehension* develops of the interpretations of the topic presented by the media.

4. Increasing comprehension among the audience of the messages supplied by the media, begins to *form* or *modify* the meanings, beliefs and attitudes that serve as guides to individual interpretation regarding the topic.

5. **Therefore**, as individual-by-individual changes in beliefs and attitudes accumulate, new shared *norms* emerge, resulting in *widespread acceptance* of audience orientations behavior toward the topic.

PUTTING IT TOGETHER: A MASTER THEORY OF EFFECTS OF MASS COMMUNICATED ENTERTAINMENT

With this final explanation concerning the time factor in place, an integrated multi-stage theory can be summarized to explain the multi-stage process by which mass communication entertainment content and related forms of popular culture are developed, delivered and come to influence youthful audiences in various countries. It is a complex process, but one that may be possible to explain in a single "master theory." That theory must bring together the various economic, demographic, production considerations, audience behavior and final outcomes that shape the beliefs and attitudes of youthful consumers of media entertainment and popular culture. To accomplish this, the theory must integrate the set of explanations, conditions and outcomes that have been presented in the previous sections of this chapter. That is, it combines the propositions of:

(1) The features of capitalism as a political and economic system based on competitions for profits, (2) the age composition of the global audience, (3) the issue of media dependence on popular culture, (4) the creeping cycle of desensitization as it shapes media entertainment content, (5) audience goals of seeking gratification from media entertainment, (6) the process of incidental learning that leads to (7) social constructions of reality by members of the audience; and finally, (8) the gradual accumulation of minimal effects taking place over time to result in the formation of beliefs and attitudes among those who selectively attend.

This, theory, then, describes a sequence of conditions and events that begins with a spark of creativity in the mind of a professional communicator, as he or she envisions the development of specific media message. It may be a movie, a TV program, a music video or another specific example of popular entertainment culture. From that beginning comes the process of designing, developing and distributing that message through a complex mass communication business with a global reach. The sequence continues when a member of an audience encounters that message, absorbs its incidental lessons and uses it to help construct his or her understanding of the nature of that which is depicted. That person's eventual construction may require many such experiences in an accumulative process. But over time, the mass media that bring popular culture to millions have served as *teachers* concerning what ordinary Americans are really like. The propositions of that integrated theory are these:

1. Making a profit is a requirement for producers in a capitalistic economic system, and to do so necessitates producing a product that will appeal to the consumers making up the relevant market.

2. For produces of media entertainment as popular culture, that market consists, for the most part, of the large and growing proportion of the world's population who are in their teenage years—whose interests and tastes are much less conservative that those of older people.

3. To satisfy that market in a highly competitive environment, producers of

media entertainment as popular culture must constantly exceed the boundaries of conservative tastes and morality in their products, stopping or retreating only when vocal critics protest strongly—and then waiting for desensitization to occur before pressing the limits forward again.

4. The products produced under the above conditions contain an abundance of incidental lessons about the people, behavior, lifestyles and conditions in societies depicted that may exceed conservative norms and be seriously flawed and misleading.

5. Those flawed incidental lessons may be unwittingly learned when audience members seek personal gratification by attending to the content of the media entertainment content that is readily available to them.

6. From exposure to those incidental lessons, members of an audience, who may lack other sources of information, develop social constructions of reality that define the nature of whatever or whomever is portrayed in the media depictions to which they attend.

7. Those constructions of reality—accurate or flawed—are a result of repeated exposures over long periods of time to similar and corroborative incidental lessons.

Generally speaking, then, this integrated theory provides an explanation of the results from the present project that were presented earlier. The young people in those societies that were studied may have little in the way of alternative sources of reliable and accurate information about Americans from which to develop their beliefs and attitudes. They do have an abundance of media depictions in the products that are distributed to them for their gratification and pleasure.

It should not be surprising, therefore, that what they believe about ordinary Americans reflects the incidental lessons embedded in those depictions, rather than the realities of life for most people in the United States.

CHAPTER ENDNOTES

1. The formal theories stated in this chapter are, in part, original in this book, and in part have been drawn from or adapted from the following publications by the authors: Melvin L. DeFleur and Everette E. Dennis, *Understanding Mass Communication*, 7th ed. (Boston: Houghton Mifflin, 2002) and also: Margaret H. DeFleur and Melvin L. DeFleur, *An Introduction to Mass Communication Theory* (Boston: Allyn and Bacon, forthcoming in 2004).

2. Adam Smith, *An Inquiry into the Nature and Causes of the Wealth of Nations* (Chicago: The University of Chicago Press, 1976). This work in various forms has been published by a number of editors, authors and interpreters since 1776.

3. *Ibid*, p. 69.

4. *Ibid*, p. 63.

5. Adam Smith, *The Theory of Moral Sentiments* (New York: Garland Press, 1971). This is a facsimile from a copy originally published in 1759.

6. See Everette E. Dennis and John C. Merrill, *Media Debates: Communication in a Digital Age* (Belmont, CA: Wadsworth, 2001).

7. Data on the compositions, trends and projections for various countries and regions of the world can be obtained from the following sources: International Programs Center: U.S. Bureau of the Census; United Nations Population Fund and Population Reference Bureau, Princeton University. An illustration of the youthful nature of developing countries is that of Iraq, where 50 percent of the population is currently less than 18 years old.

8. See: "Europe's Population Implosion," *The Economist*, July 19, 2003, p. 42.

9. Herbert J. Gans, *Popular Culture and High Culture* (New York: Basic Books, 1975), p. 10.

10. These details were supplied to the authors by graduate students who are residents of Pakistan, and who are familiar with the culture and ways of life in rural areas of that country. Others, from countries with similar levels of development, describe much the same arrangements in their countries.

11. This theory first appeared in Melvin L. DeFleur and Everette E. Dennis, *Understanding Mass Communication,* 5th ed. (Boston: Houghton Mifflin, 1994).

12. See Albert Bandura and Robert H. Walters, *Social Learning and Personality Development* (New York: McGraw Hill, 1962).

13. Wilbur Schramm, Jack Lyle and Edwin B. Parker, *Television in the Lives of Our Children* (Stanford, CA: Stanford University Press, 1961), p. 75.

14. Madeline A. Dalton, *et. al.* Effect of Smoking in Movies on Adolescent Smoking Imitation: A Cohort Study. *Lancet*, 361, 9273, June 2003. (This was a cooperative study conducted by eight colleagues. This citation is the online version.)

15. *The Republic of Plato*, trans. Francis MacDonald Cornfield (New York: Oxford University Press, 1958). See pp. 227-35. Plato's work was written in 387 B.C.

16. See Walter Lippmann, *Public Opinion* (New York: MacMillan, 1920).

CHAPTER 7

IMPLICATIONS FOR THE FUTURE

Three perspectives are important in understanding the implications and consequences for Americans of what has been found in the present project. Given the fact that many young people studied in the most of the societies discussed in this report have at least some flawed and negative feelings a about ordinary Americans, what does that fact imply for the future?

One way to answer that question is to use a *political* perspective. The most central concern of this perspective is the possibility of future acts of terrorism, either in the United States or in other areas of the world where Americans are located. Almost without exception, such acts are committed by young people who see the United States and its people as their enemy. A second answer is to use a *public health* perspective. This raises the issue as to whether the country's present concern with terrorism will decline or continue over the years ahead. If it continues, there is likely to be an extension of the stresses and anxieties that currently characterize at least some segments of the American population.

Finally, the third answer is provided by an *economic* perspective. The issue here is that if those of the each new generation, in countries such as those studied, hold negative views of Americans, that fact could lead to a reduction in their willingness to import products and services from the United States. If that happens, the current very favorable economic position in the world market place that the United States enjoys would be eroded.

ROLE OF YOUTH IN ACTS OF TERRORISM: A POLITICAL PERSPECTIVE

Most negative incidents that take place in a country where Americans are present are not enough to spark and generate a "culture of hate." On the contrary, as noted earlier, widespread denunciation of a negative incident by a population appears to rest upon a *prior condition*—a pre-existing complex of negative beliefs and attitudes toward the people of the United States and their government, such as that found in the present project.

Thus, a basic assumption upon which the present study rests is this: *The collective condemnation expressed by a people when a negative incident occurs does not come out of nowhere.* As a general principle, then, a negative incident can become a *cause celebre,* rallying widespread anger, only if a necessary condition is met. Specifically, *there must already be in place a foundation of shared negative beliefs and attitudes toward the United States upon which the feelings generated by the specific incident can be based.*

But what are those conditions? The importance of a significant negative incident was discussed in Chapter 2. These occurrences are almost inevitable in countries where there is an American presence—particularly a military one. Accidents, as well as deliberate acts and crimes will happen. These can always be used by organizations or others with grudges against Americans to arouse strong negative feelings about the people of the United States.

However, it was also suggested that such an incident in itself is *a necessary but not a sufficient condition* to provoke drastic actions. Public demonstrations can take place, flags may be burned, fists may be shaken and chants can denounce the United States, but those acts do not inevitably lead to youthful terrorism.

Given recent history, it appears that other conditions must be present to provoke bombings and similar destructive acts. One possibility is that a religious factor may serve as a necessary condition for some. That seems to be supported by the fact that the terrorists that most concern the United States today are Muslims. But extreme caution must be exercised in making such an interpretation. Religion is *certainly not a sufficient condition.* It is well understood that the overwhelming majority of members of the Muslim faith pose no threats whatever to anyone. Indeed, there are grounds for assuming that the Muslim faith has been "hijacked" by those who are using it to bolster their political agendas.

At the same time, it is clear that religion must be considered. That is, although it may seem unfair to point the finger at Muslims in discussing such problems, this factor among a small minority has played an important part in recent acts of terrorism. In contrast, however, few terrorists have come from non-Muslim South Korea, Mexico, Taiwan or other countries where negative feelings about Americans clearly exist among some young people. In terms of logical analysis, then, a religious factor does not appear to be, in itself, a necessary condition of today's terrorism by militant groups.

What, then, is also needed to enable those committed to terrorism to arouse young people to engage in hostile acts? That principle was stated earlier in the following terms:

> *There must already be in place a foundation of shared negative beliefs and attitudes toward the people of the United States upon which the feelings generated by the specific incident can be based.*

In other words, the condition of commonly shared *negative evaluations of Americans*—as illustrated by the findings from the present project—appear to provide a third necessary (but not sufficient) condition that can increase the likelihood of harm to the people of the United States.

Even so, if all three of the above conditions are present, one cannot assume that young people will automatically be persuaded to engage in hostile actions. However, if all four necessary conditions are present—negative incidents, the religious factor, a foundation of negative beliefs and attitudes, plus the presence of militant groups who recruit youths—those conditions, taken together, appear to make up a *sufficient multi-condition.* If that is the case, and that sufficient multi-condition is present, the probability of at least some young people being recruited to engage in terrorist acts will be high.[1]

Those four conditions do appear to be present in countries such as Saudi-Arabia and Bahrain. In contrast, as Figure 1 indicates, in such countries as Nigeria, Italy and Argentina, none of the four appear to be present. As a consequence, there seems little possibility that young people from those countries will be recruited by militant groups to engage in hostile acts against Americans.

In general, then, if the results of the present project can be considered at all representative and valid, there appears to be a significant probability that the threat of terrorist acts against Americans *will continue in the years ahead.* In those countries where the four necessary conditions come together to form a *sufficient multi-condition*, it seems likely that at least some from each new generation will be recruited and trained to engage in terrorism against what they will define as their enemy. If that is indeed the case, the United States will be likely to remain embroiled for many years in a political struggle to contain terrorism, both at home and abroad.

TERRORISM THREATS AND STRESSES ON AMERICANS:
A PUBLIC HEALTH PERSPECTIVE

There have obviously been changes in American life since September 11, 2001. Many of those changes have brought concerns, anxieties and fears to many citizens that they did not have before that date. National outrage and mourning for those lost in the World Trade Center and the Pentagon has been one source of distress. Another is the constant alerts and warnings in the news about possible terrorist activities. A third is news reports and public discussions about Al-Qeda, regrouping of the Taliban, speculation about Osama Bin Ladin, the whereabouts of Saddam Hussein, the prospects for enemies developing weapons of mass destruction and possible policies, actions and decisions that may be needed to preempt their use.

All of these do little to alleviate national concerns. Anyone who has traveled on an airliner in recent times has seen visible indicators that danger still exists. It is not only the additional inconvenience of standing in line, showing identification repeatedly, or the body and luggage searches, but the realization of how truly vulnerable a jet aircraft is if terrorists successfully find their way on board.

Viewed in this perspective, continuing sources of anxiety over possible hostile acts of terrorism constitutes *a public health problem*. It is not unreasonable to assume that it is one that is unlikely to go away if the young people in many countries continue to have decidedly negative attitudes and beliefs about Americans. If these views do indeed provide the suggested foundation of beliefs enabling leaders of hostile groups to recruit and train the young for terrorist purposes, then Americans have solid grounds for their concerns.

Unfortunately, as the present findings suggest, that may indeed be the case, and the American people are likely to remain in harm's way. Given these conditions, it is unlikely that the country, or its people, will return to the more relaxed way of life that existed before September 11, 2001.

NEGATIVE ATTITUDES AND THE MARKETPLACE:
AN ECONOMIC PERSPECTIVE

As noted earlier, the economy of the United States has no current equal. As we also noted earlier, if the GDPs all nations on earth are combined, a third of everything that is produced and brought to market on the globe comes from the United States—even though it has only 4.7 percent of the world's population.

The American stock and bond market traditionally provides investment opportunities for people in many countries. In addition, the United States is by any measure far ahead of any other country in the issuance of patents, and in expenditures of research and development. For that reason it is likely to maintain economic world leadership in the future, in spite of temporary business cycles. Another reason is that the official policies of the United States are designed to increase world trade and open markets on the grounds that this is a sound strategy for bolstering the American economy.

What could happen if a substantial number of people in the world decide that they no longer want American investments, goods and services? That may seem unlikely, given the current dominance enjoyed by the United States. But the findings revealed by the present study are troublesome in that they suggest a different state of affairs could be possible in the future.

Specifically, that segment of the world's population who are now teenagers represents the next generation of decision-making adults. Within a decade they will be the ones who are parents and heads of families, the ones who manage businesses, the ones who become influential in government—and above all—who make economic decisions at all levels. If their current dislike of Americans continues into their adult years, there may be more at stake than the prospect of more incidents of terrorism. Moreover, that situation not only applies the specific generation studied in the present project, but those oncoming population cohorts who will soon enough become teenagers—and then adults.

A significant factor that would seem to minimize a decline in the acceptance of American investments, goods and services is that for many people in the world those products seem highly desirable. Even with temporary changes in comparative values, dollar-based investments will probably remain highly regarded in comparison to those in other currencies. People worldwide eagerly acquire our latest entertainment products, our manufactured goods, and many other things that Americans produce.

Yet, as globalization in the production of consumer goods, financial services and other aspects of economies continues—a policy actively supported by the United States—there will be increasing competition on all fronts. Added to the fact that goods now obtained from the United States may in the future be cheaper if obtained elsewhere, and if there continues to be widespread negative attitudes and beliefs about Americans, there could be unwanted economic consequences.

PROSPECTS FOR CHANGE

What the present results do not provide is a clear strategy to change the views of Americans among young people in other countries to make them more favorable. Achieving such a goal would be a daunting challenge, to say the least.

Communication scholars know that altering beliefs and attitudes about others that have already formed can be very difficult. Racial and gender-preference stereotypes are a case in point. Beliefs and attitudes are stable features of what psychologists refer to as one's "cognitive structure." Once established, they make life easy for us, and we truly need them.

In a complex daily environment, people must use quick and simple ways of evaluating objects or people that they encounter in order to respond to them. Even our earliest initial impressions of people—the kind that we form almost instantly when we first meet someone—are based on only a few visible and salient characteristics that we quickly observe—and even these are stubbornly resistant to change. Impressions established over a longer period, and based on repeated experiences with a person, or a category of persons, are much more difficult to modify. Yet, these difficulties do not mean that no such effort should be made.

If the conclusions of the present project are correct, however, such change appears unlikely. Incidental lessons are likely to be repeatedly embedded in media entertainment content and popular culture. These appear to serve as sources for long-term development of negative social constructions of reality concerning the nature of Americans on the part of teenage audiences. If that is indeed the case, only significant change *in those lessons themselves* would provide a basis for change.

Suppose, however, that those who design, develop and disseminate movies, TV programs, music videos, computer games and all the rest, decided to listen to their "inner man" who tells them that they should stop using in their products such themes as violence, sex and crime to depict Americans. What would happen?

If Adam Smith was correct, they would go broke! However, one can ask, why not also use more positive themes of equal appeal to attract the interest of and amuse teenagers around the world? If they did that, new generations of teenagers could have less negative views of the people who live in the United States.

But what are those themes, and would they bring in profits? Earlier media entertainment products used such themes as wholesome family situation dramas—with well-scrubbed teenagers, dads going off to work with the brief case in hand and mom at staying home to take care of domestic tasks and problems.

Obviously, few Americans still live in that world. Or, how about Tarzan, or Disney characters, such as Flipper, and other animal themes? They were widely used to entertain the young.

Unfortunately, to teenagers today, who are accustomed to much racier and exciting fare, that kind of content would probably seem vapid and dated. They are more attracted to lots of fast action, graphic violence, open sex, crime and coarse language. In other words, once a preference is created for that kind of content, few other options may now be available in any real (market driven) sense to those who produce media entertainment. For that reason, the process described in the creeping cycle of desensitization theory probably provides a more accurate view of what lies ahead—rather than a retreat to the wholesome themes of the past.

Another barrier to revamping what teenagers in other countries learn about Americans is the First Amendment of the U.S. Constitution. When it was first set forth, as the nation was formed, it was a means of protecting *political* speech. It allowed those who disagreed with policies and decisions made by government, or by private groups in the society, to voice their discontent in the press, or in speech, without fear of retaliation. In that sense, it served the people of the United States well. Indeed it still does.

Today, because of that Amendment, the United States is a "transparent" society to a degree enjoyed by few others in the world, and most Americans approve heartily. Even if the highest of government officials engages in embarrassing acts of sexual indiscretion, the public ultimately learns about it. Even if powerful corporations engage in unethical dealings and deceptive practices that they seek to cover up, the news media let people know. Obviously, that is a situation that few Americans would want to abandon.

However, in the more than two centuries since the First Amendment became a reality, its protections have been extended to many other forms of communication that seem difficult to define as "political." Today, what was earlier considered unacceptable pornography, is also protected. With a few key strokes one can download content from the Internet that would have caused riots in earlier times. One routinely sees frontal nudity and depictions of naked people coupling in many movies. The vocabulary of many actors on contemporary TV would have characterized only the most foul-mouthed thugs of earlier years. Therefore to suggest that the government should now begin to monitor and censor the way Americans are depicted in media entertainment content and popular culture would be unrealistic and an exercise in futility.

A potential strategy to limit the flow of flawed depictions of Americans to audiences around the world would be to persuade those who prepare and disseminate popular culture and media entertainment products to "clean up their act." on a voluntary basis. They could be asked to listen more closely to the "inner man" (as described by Adam Smith) who monitors the decisions that they make—including those of preparing and disseminating harmful portrayals of Americans.

That may sound unrealistic, but a version of that was actually done within the movie industry many decades ago. In the face of public pressure and widespread objections to movie content depicting crime, violence and sexual content in the late 1920s and early 1930s, the industry developed the Motion Picture Producers and Distributors Code. It spelled out in almost puritanical detail how scenes and people were to be depicted so as to meet the public's beliefs as to what was acceptable within the norms of the time. Motion pictures that did not meet its requirements were not allowed in theaters (that were largely owned by the producer companies at the time).[2] In the face of competition from television, and declining box office receipts, the code was largely abandoned over the decades since.

However, the likelihood that such a code, or other efforts of persuasion for voluntary action, would take care of the current problem is probably near zero. The competition for profits is intense. Those who control and operate such media production enterprises are, after all, locked into the forces and laws of the "invisible hand" governing the capitalistic marketplace.

They are not members of an "evil empire," deliberately setting out to harm Americans. Just as is the case with the fast food industry that produces products and portions that contribute to obesity, they are responding to economic rules over which they have little or no control. When content producers are asked why they have persisted in preparing and exporting products that create harm, their reply is (as Jack Valenti noted in commenting on one news report of this study) "We are just giving people what they want." Presumably, that is also the case for those who provide huge servings in restaurants, giant hamburgers or rich milk shakes. They, too, are "just giving people what they want." To stop offering that level of "quality" in their goods would mean losing their markets.

In addition to those considerations for producers and distributors, there is in this situation, an important but long-range ethical implication for higher education. It is particularly relevant to those who teach in communication programs, departments and schools where students are taught to make movies, televison programs and other forms of popular culture.

Should such educators train students to *avoid* producing films and television dramas that include incidental lessons defining Americans in pejorative terms? Specifically, should their students make films or produce TV dramas to be sent abroad that increasingly follow the "creeping cycle" process? Is it ethical to teach young people in a number of other societies through incidental lessons to loath ordinary Americans? If the answer is "yes," then for succeeding generations in many countries, media content will be continue to be a factor in the development of their attitudes toward Americans.

What the future holds concerning these issues is anyone's guess. It is not possible to make accurate forecasts about the probability of acts of terrorism, or any other consequence, based solely on the information derived from the present project. Mark Twain is said to have noted that "forecasting can be difficult—especially when it concerns the future."

However, one thing can be foreseen: There is every reason to believe that (unless changes are made) as each new generation ages in countries around the world that receive and enjoy the popular culture produced in the United States, those generations too will learn to judge Americans from what they encounter in their media entertainment experiences. There is little doubt that those judgments may be formed in part by what they learn about the foreign policies, military actions, and so forth of the United States as a government. They may also be influenced by their religious instruction.

However, a case has been made in this project that another important influence shaping their views concerning the people who live in the United States will be the incidental lessons that they receive while seeing Americans depicted in movies and TV dramas. In short, if what has been set forth in this report can be confirmed by additional studies, it is not that difficult to understand what is implied if no changes are made in the process of designing, developing and distributing media entertainment products produced in the United States. The U.S. media will continue to serve as *weapons of mass instruction,* shaping flawed and negative beliefs about and interpretations of the moral and behavioral nature of ordinary Americans in the decades ahead. Stated more explicitly:

If mass media products distributed globally continue to include, or increase, the kinds of negative and flawed incidental lessons concerning the nature of ordinary Americans that are now embedded in their content, oncoming generations in countries around the world will continue unwittingly to learn those lessons with potentially harmful consequences to the people of the United States.

Thus, the most important feature of the findings of this project is not so much that (at a particular point in time) the young people in the countries studied entertained negative beliefs and attitudes concerning the people who live in the

United States. That was not particularly surprising. What does seem important is that oncoming future generations will continue to enjoy and learn from the media-delivered popular culture depicting Americans that is currently developed and exported worldwide.

Obviously, to confirm such a conclusion, a much greater foundation of research findings is badly needed. Media scholars have over many decades assembled a vast set of findings—literally thousands of studies—indicating that at least some American children can be influenced in negative ways by the content of the mass media.

Scholars now need to turn their attention to the extent of the harm that our globally distributed media entertainment appear to be creating among young people who do not live in the United States. The issue of what role the media are playing will not be settled by claims and counterclaims derived from Marxian or other ideologies. What is needed is a body of carefully assembled facts focusing on the issue explored in this project.

However, if the explanations and interpretations discussed here are indeed supported, and no changes are made, it is not difficult to anticipate what will happen. Future cohorts of teenagers in many countries will be exposed to even more negative depictions of Americans. If that indeed is the case, and the other three necessary conditions (as discussed earlier) are present, there will be no cessation of hostilities perpetrated by those who despise the United States and who have learned from incidental lessons provided by entertainment media to loath its people.

CHAPTER ENDNOTES

1. This set of conditions is not exclusive to the American situation. In May of 2003, officials in Saudi Arabia uncovered a plot to bomb the holy city of Mecca. The terrorist groups planning the incidents were able to recruit individuals as young as 15. Three were 17 and one 18. More than half of the Saudi population is under 18. See: Faiiza Salah Ambah, "Suspects in Saudi Terror Plot Reportedly Include Teens," *The Boston Globe,* June 23, 2003.

2. Melvin L. DeFleur and Everette E. Dennis, "Cleaning Up the Movies," *Understanding Mass Communication,* 7th ed. (Boston: Houghton Mifflin, 2002), pp. 149-155.

INDEX

A

ABC, 21
accumulation of minimal effects, 103, 105, 106
Afghanistan, 16, 32
Age of Popular Culture, 89
Allegory of the Cave, 100
American people, 15, 33, 51, 83, 114
AOL Time Warner, 23, 24
Argentina, 13, 51, 54, 55, 74, 113
artifact, 72, 73
attitude object, 17, 35-41, 68
Attitude Scale, 37, 43, 51, 55, 68, 71-73
attitudes, 13, 15-19, 22, 28, 31-33, 35, 36, 38, 40-43, 45, 51-55, 68, 73, 74, 83, 84, 99, 102-107, 112-116, 119
attitudes toward America, 38
audiences, 14, 16, 20-22, 24, 25, 42, 43, 69, 73, 77, 83, 87, 88, 92-95, 97-99, 105, 116, 117

B

Bagdad, 32, 42
Bahrain, 13, 20, 51, 52, 55, 74, 113
Bandura, Albert, 108
Baywatch, 15
beliefs, 13, 15-19, 22, 30-33, 35-38, 40, 41, 43, 45, 52-55, 68, 73, 74, 83, 84, 97, 99, 102-107, 112-116, 118, 119
Bertelsmann AG, 23
birth rate, 73
Bosnia, 16
Boston, 11, 16, 20, 32, 36, 38, 77, 91, 113, 118

Bush, George, 27

C

Capital Cities, 21
capitalism, 13, 78, 93, 106
capitalistic system, 77, 79, 94, 98
Catton, William R., 43
change, 29, 30, 37, 68, 115, 116
Chicago, 24, 78, 90
China, 13, 54, 55, 68, 74, 85
Christians, 31, 32
CIA, 46
collective condemnation, 33, 112
communication scholars, 77, 116
competition, 14, 79-81, 92, 93, 115, 118
conspiracy, 30, 31
Constitution, 93, 117
Cornfield, Francis MacDonald, 109
correlation, 69-73
cultural diffusion, 30
cultural imperialism, 30
culture of hate, 27, 28, 33, 111
cycle of desensitization, 93, 94, 106, 117

D

Dalton, Madeline A., 109
DeFleur, Margaret, 9-10, 26, 108
DeFleur, Melvin, 9-10, 26, 43-44, 108, 120
Demers, David, 10, 21, 23
demographers, 85, 86
Dennis, Everette, 108, 120
desensitization, 93, 94, 106, 107, 117
desensitized, 93
developed countries, 85-88

developing countries, 86-88
Disney, 21, 23, 116
disposable income, 87-89
DVD, 14

E

economic conditions, 77, 79
economic dependency, 91
economic perspective, 111, 114
economic system, 13, 21, 78, 91, 106
evaluative beliefs, 36-38, 68, 74, 103

F

false view of reality, 101
fascism, 54

G

Gans, Herbert, 108
GDP, 28
General Electric, 21
Gerbner, George 9
Germany, 27, 87
global market, 24, 81, 86, 92
global media, 10, 20, 21, 79, 81, 83, 84
globalization, 40, 115
Gross Domestic Product, 28

H

Haiti, 16
Hitler, Adolf, 27
human nature, 82

I

incidental learning, 73, 96-98, 106
Industrial Revolution, 78, 80, 89
institutions, 48, 82
internal knowledge, 100
internal spectator, 81, 82

Iraq, 16-18, 32, 40, 86
Italy, 13, 51, 54, 87, 113

J

Japan, 28

K

Kamalipour, Yahya, 21, 26
Kipling, 29, 34, 52-54
kitsch, 91, 92
Kyoto Treaty, 17

L

Lebanon, 13, 16
leisure time, 89, 91
Likert, Rensis, 35, 44
Likert scale, 35, 37, 38, 41, 42, 47, 68
Lippmann, Walter, 109
Lyle, Jack, 109

M

market, 14, 20, 24, 28, 78-81, 84-86, 92, 94,
    106, 111, 114, 115, 117
marketplace, 32, 78, 79, 81, 82, 114, 118
Marx, Karl, 84, 120
mass communication, 9, 21, 23, 77, 84, 88,
    90, 91, 94, 99, 102, 104-106, 118
mass media, 9, 10, 13, 21, 23-25, 40, 43, 74,
    79, 84, 88, 89, 96, 103, 105, 106, 119,
    120
maximizing profits, 83
Media Influences Subscale, 68, 70-72, 74
media scholars, 21, 84, 120
Merrill, John C., 108
Mexico, 13, 24, 52-54, 68, 74, 112
moral codes, 40, 41
motivations, 18, 77, 82
multinational corporations, 13, 14, 20-23, 83,
    88, 96

Muslims, 27, 31, 32, 38, 54, 74, 112

N

National Broadcasting Company, 23
negative incident, 32, 33, 112
News Corporation, The, 23
news stories, 22
news values, 22, 69
Nigeria, 13, 51, 54, 113
norms, 14, 82, 93, 94, 105, 107, 118

O

opinion polls, 33
Oskamp, Stuart, 44

P

Pakistan, 13, 20, 54, 55, 68, 90
Parker, Edwin B., 109
Pentagon, 28, 114
People's Republic of China, The, 54
Pew Research Center, 16, 40
Plato, 82, 99-102
political perspective, 111
popular culture, 13, 14, 17, 19-25, 31, 40-43, 68, 74, 75, 80, 81, 83-95, 99, 104-107, 116-119
population pyramids, 86
profit-making, 84, 88
public health, 16, 111, 114

Q

quality (perceived quality of media products), 80, 81, 83, 88, 92-94, 97, 118

R

religion, 31, 32, 51, 52, 73, 112
Republic, The, 54, 100

S

Saudi Arabia, 13, 74, 83, 102, 113
Schramm, Wilbur, 96, 109
sensory experience, 100, 101
Smith, Adam, 13, 31, 78-84, 88, 92, 103, 116, 117
social construction of reality, 99, 101-103
social learning, 96
Somalia, 16
Sony, 23
South Korea, 13, 20, 32, 52-54, 74, 83, 112
Spain, 13, 74
sufficient multi-condition, 113
superpower, 28

T

Taiwan, 13, 54, 74, 112
television/TV, 9, 13-17, 19-21, 23-24, 31, 33, 41-43, 48, 68, 69, 74, 80, 88-90, 94-97, 99, 102, 104, 106, 116-119
television programming, 21, 31, 33, 68, 97, 99
terrorism, 16, 28, 40, 111-115, 119
The Sopranos, 15
Theory of Moral Sentiments, 82, 83
Thompson Corporation, 23
Time Warner, 21, 23, 24

U

U.S. government, 19, 30, 31, 35, 52
United Nations, 86
United States, 9, 10, 13-19, 22, 23, 27-33, 38-41, 43, 45-48, 52-54, 69, 72-75, 82, 88, 90, 93, 94, 99, 104, 107, 111-117, 119, 120
Uses for Gratification Theory, 95

V

VCR, 20, 41, 42, 87-90
Viacom, 23
violence, 9, 16, 22, 42, 68, 72, 81, 92-94, 116-118

Vivendi Universal, 23, 24

W

Walt Disney Company, The, 23
Walters, 96
Wealth of Nations, 78, 81

weapons of mass destruction, 114
weapons of mass instruction, 119
Western countries, 87
Westie, Frank R., 43, 44
World Trade Center, 16, 27, 114
World War II, 18, 27, 54